THE PEOPLE'S RIGHTS

We are going into battle.
Let us stand together like comrades and brothers.
The issues are very simple, but they are very great.
We have to drive the Budget through.
We have to smash the veto up, and if we march together
there is none that can withstand us.

THE
PEOPLE'S
RIGHTS

BY THE RIGHT HON.
WINSTON SPENCER CHURCHILL, M.P.

President of the Board of Trade

INTRODUCTION BY CAMERON HAZLEHURST

TAPLINGER PUBLISHING COMPANY
NEW YORK

FIRST PUBLISHED IN THE UNITED STATES IN 1971 BY
TAPLINGER PUBLISHING CO., INC.
NEW YORK, NEW YORK
INTRODUCTION COPYRIGHT © 1970 BY CAMERON HAZLEHURST

ISBN 0 8008 6278 3
Library of Congress Catalog Card Number 71 137661

PRINTED IN GREAT BRITAIN

INTRODUCTION

The People's Rights was compiled and published at great speed in the last weeks of 1909. It was designed, as the author explained, 'as a guide for some and as an armoury for others' in the general election campaign which followed the rejection of the 1909 Budget by the Conservative majority in the House of Lords. Winston Churchill's agreement with Messrs Hodder and Stoughton specified that two editions of the work, originally entitled *The People's Rights Defended*, would be published. For the cheap edition, to be sold at one shilling, Churchill was guaranteed a ten per cent royalty; on the two-shilling edition he was to receive fifteen per cent. An advance of one hundred pounds was paid on the signature of the contract. The first copies of the book reached the bookstalls in the second week of January 1910 and were quickly sold. There was no reprint; and in 1969 sixty pounds was paid for a second-hand copy in good condition.

Churchill distilled the six chapters of *The People's Rights* from a series of brilliant speeches, most of them delivered in Lancashire in the first fortnight of December 1909. The last of the speeches was delivered on December 12th. Four days later, J. E. Hodder-Williams, the chairman of Hodder and Stoughton, wrote to Churchill:

As you suggested, we are making up the book into page form. The printers have been most careful, and have

suggested various deletions of repeated matter, so I
think you can safely leave it in our hands, but of course
I am sending you page proofs as soon as possible.

Neither the printers' vigilance, nor Churchill's own scru-
tiny of the proofs, removed all the repetitive passages:
occasional references to particular audiences and occasions
survived, and are reproduced in this edition. Many sections
retain the characteristic flavour of platform rhetoric. But,
hurried and imperfect though it was, the book was a powerful plea for both constitutional reform and 'a great policy of
social reconstruction and reorganization'.

What gave the book its strength? First, the careful preparation on which its economic arguments were based. Two
weeks before he began the Lancashire tour, Churchill addressed a memorandum to the Commercial Department of
his ministry, the Board of Trade:

1. I am going to speak in Lancashire from the 2nd to
   the 12th December, visiting Manchester, Preston,
   Southport, Liverpool, Bolton, Burnley, Oldham,
   Crewe and perhaps Wirral. Please let me have a note
   on the trade and labour conditions in each of these
   towns, the special industries, their state at the present
   time, new industries or mills recently started, and any
   other matter which may strike you as likely to be
   useful to me.
2. Prepare me some statistics dealing with the British
   and German cotton industries, showing their respec-
   tive size, exports to protected and neutral markets,
   growth by value, by bulk and by spindles, etc.
3. Let me have a short note on the trade of Lancashire
   as a whole.
4. Compare the trade activity of Lancashire, exports,

imports, etc., per head of the population with the trade activity of great protected countries.

5. If an average 10 per cent were imposed on imports of foreign manufacturers mention what articles or categories of articles would be included in schedules which are used in the cotton industry. To what extent are flour and leather used?

This will not be wanted until the middle of next week.

18.11.9.   W.S.C.

In answer to the President of the Board of Trade's precise and comprehensive requests, his officials supplied a formidable brief. Churchill digested the inch-thick file of statistics and analysis, and laced his speeches with apposite calculations and examples. However, it was not the thorough verification of his defence of free trade that most distinguished Churchill's case. Other Liberal orators — Alexander Ure and Russell Rea, for example — were equally versed in the traditional radical arguments and their statistical proofs. Churchill's unique contribution was the blending of hallowed precepts with new and optimistic proposals for managing the economy and improving 'the people's welfare'. Rejecting gloomy orthodoxy on unemployment, for example, he argued:

There is nothing economically unsound in increasing temporarily and artificially the demand for labour during a period of temporary and artificial contraction. There is a plain need of some averaging machinery to regulate and even-up the general course of the labour market, in the same way as the Bank of England, by its bank rate, regulates and corrects the flow of business enterprise. When the extent of the depression is foreseen, the extent of the relief should also be determined.

Twenty years before the onset of the great depression, and thirty years before the idea of counter-cyclical public expenditure had achieved any significant measure of acceptance, Churchill here appealed for a concerted effort to 'reduce the oscillation of the industrial system'. There were many to applaud his phrases, none yet to translate them into reality.

Soon after composing these words, Churchill left the Board of Trade for the Home Office, where fresh responsibilities soon dominated his attention. He had first publicly outlined his ideas on combating unemployment in October 1908 at Dundee. Eight months later he presented a tentative, but detailed, plan to the Chancellor of the Exchequer, David Lloyd George. No evidence of Lloyd George's response to Churchill's proposals has survived. There is no reason to suppose that he would have been less than enthusiastic. But, in Churchill's scheme, the functions of gathering information and forecasting the scale of unemployment were assigned to the Board of Trade. And Churchill's successor as President, Sidney Buxton, lacked both the stature and acumen to carry through so daring a proposal, even if he had supported it.

The occasion which prompted the publication of *The People's Rights* is one of the best-known episodes in British political history. Since 1906 the Liberal Government had been frustrated by a hostile majority in the Upper House. Licensing, Education, and Scottish Smallholding Bills had foundered in the Lords. Legislation to abolish plural voting was also blocked. But not until the rejection of the Budget of 1909 did the Government find an issue on which to fight. Who was to rule? Six hundred Lords or six million voters? That was the question that was put to the voters who were forced to the polls because of the denial of supplies to the Crown.

Churchill's aim in *The People's Rights* was to provide a comprehensive summary of the Liberal case for the election. But his speeches in 1909 and earlier had inevitably touched upon enduring problems and appealed to basic principles. Underlying all the arguments in *The People's Rights* was one fundamental political objective: the raising of the welfare of the people. As early as 1899, Churchill had told his cousin, Ivor Guest: 'The improvement of the British breed is my political aim in life.' In the same year, he put 'the improvement of the condition of the British people' in the forefront of his address to the electors at the Oldham by-election. Perhaps these phrases were, originally, merely a contrived echo of his father's Tory democracy. But they soon became something more. 'National efficiency' was an increasingly fashionable creed, and the welfare of the working classes the subject of intensive investigation. Just before Christmas 1901, the Liberal John Morley recommended that Churchill should read Seebohm Rowntree's newly published book *Poverty: A Study of Town Life*. Rowntree's analysis impressed the young Tory who wrote in a private letter:

It is quite evident from the figures he adduces that the American labourer is a stronger, larger, healthier, better fed, and consequently more efficient animal than a large proportion of our population ... What is wanted is a well-balanced policy midway between the Hotel Cecil and Exeter Hall, something that will co-ordinate development and expansion with the progress of social comfort and health.

The policy, which neither the 'Hotel Cecil' (Lord Salisbury's Conservative administration) nor Exeter Hall's humanitarian supporters of overseas missionary endeavour seemed willing to devise, was promoted after 1906 by the radical wing of the Liberal Party. From May 1908 Churchill, with Lloyd George, formed the Cabinet vanguard of advanced Liberalism. They urged upon Asquith, the Prime Minister, what Churchill called 'a tremendous policy in Social Organization'. In December 1908, Churchill listed for the Prime Minister the steps which he believed would begin the transformation of British life:

1. Labour Exchanges and Unemployed Insurance:
2. National Infirmity Insurance, etc:
3. Special Expansive State Industries-Afforestation-Roads:
4. Modernized Poor Law, i.e. classification:
5. Railway Amalgamation with State Control and guarantee:
6. Education compulsory till seventeen.

It was a large programme. And, in advancing major proposals over so wide a range, Churchill was conscious both of the magnitude of the imaginative leap which he was asking his colleagues to make, and of the apparent temerity required of a thirty-four-year-old minister who proposed such a leap. As he wrote of another matter to Lord Crewe in June 1909, he had 'a full sense of the fallibility of one's own judgment, especially in regard to matters which one does not watch from day to day with direct personal responsibility'.

Nevertheless, by December 1909, the Cabinet had aligned itself behind the greater part of the Churchillian reform programme. The President of the Board of Trade was able to tell his Lancashire audiences with justifiable pride: 'We have left the wilderness of phrases and formulas, the cut and dried party issues, and we have broken violently into a world of constructive action.'

What had been achieved, and what was still promised, by the end of 1909, was described in *The Crisis of Liberalism* by the radical, J. A. Hobson, as 'a vigorous, definite, positive policy of social reconstruction, involving important modifications in the legal and economic institutions of private property and private industry.' But it was not a revolution. Churchill himself, perhaps unconsciously, remained partly imprisoned by the ideas of an earlier generation. He believed in the progressive evolution of society through the beneficent operation of competitive selection. 'That system', he said, 'is one which offers an almost indefinite capacity for improvement.' But Churchill recognized that the system was not perfect. Free competition upwards was healthy; but free competition downwards was intolerable. As early as October 1906, he had publicly proclaimed his belief that the state should increasingly assume the role of the 'reserve employer' of labour. And where unemployment, sickness, and old age threatened the security of the working man, he sought to 'spread a net over the abyss'.

The application of 'scientific' organization seemed to Churchill to offer a way forward in industrial and social life. Both he and Lloyd George were deeply impressed by the methodical activities of the German government in the field of social welfare. 'I say,' he told the Prime Minister in December 1908, 'thrust a big slice of Bismarckianism over the whole underside of our industrial system, and await the consequences, whatever they may be, with a good conscience.' Of course, it would be a mistake to suppose that, in advocating Bismarckianism, Churchill's motivation came entirely from a sensitive social conscience. There was also some party advantage — though less than is sometimes believed — to be won from compassion and reforming enthusiasm. But at the root of Churchill's concern it is possible to perceive a lurking fear. It was a fear that the failure of the government to satisfy the aspirations of a democratic

electorate would sharpen antagonisms and introduce a
disastrous era of class warfare. He wrote:

> If we stand on in the old happy-go-lucky way, the
> richer classes ever growing in wealth and in number,
> and ever declining in responsibility, the very poor
> remaining plunged or plunging even deeper into help-
> less, hopeless misery, then I think there is nothing
> before us but savage strife between class and class.

The unprecedented action of the House of Lords in
throwing out a Liberal Budget could be seen as a deliberate
incitement to the kind of struggle which Churchill professed
himself anxious to prevent. On the one hand, Liberal propagandists put the matter this way:

> The question for every thoughtful voter is ... shall the
> people, in matters of finance, be governed by the Lords,
> or shall they retain their right to govern themselves?
> If you think they should govern themselves, through
> the House of Commons which they elect,
> SUPPORT THE PEOPLE'S RIGHTS AND THE
>   PEOPLE'S BUDGET.

In reply, the peers denounced Lloyd George's increases in
income-tax and death duties, and the new plans for land
taxation as 'socialistic', 'vindictive', 'penal', and 'iniquitous'.
Churchill defined the issue as whether the new taxation—
which everyone agreed was essential to pay for Old-Age
Pensions and naval construction—should be imposed upon
'luxuries, superfluities, and monopolies, or upon the prime
necessaries of life'. In a fiercely controversial election campaign, it was scarcely possible to avoid a clear and partisan
definition of the issue. But *The People's Rights* reminds us
that Churchill's convictions and exuberance sometimes
carried him further than he intended. On the platform, the

suggestion of a smile could take the edge off extravagant sarcasm and personal invective. But even in a hall packed with cotton-operatives it was surely dangerous for a minister of the Crown to brand his Conservative opponents in the House of Lords as 'utterly unfit to have any concern with serious affairs'. Moreover, in cold print, such phrases took on a deadly life of their own.

It was one of the ironies of Churchill's career that, by the very fluency and remorselessness of his own attacks on land monopoly and Protectionism, he undermined the foundation of the political system which he strove to preserve. The more sharply focused the wealthy Conservative enemy became, the greater was the drift away from the sanity of Liberalism into the extremes of class antagonism. In using the dread of future class warfare as a political weapon in 1909, Churchill and his Liberal colleagues helped to unleash powerful forces. Perhaps the emergence of a strong Labour Party was inevitable. But by invoking the Socialist spectre, the Liberals unintentionally hastened a political transformation which they were to prove incapable of controlling.

In the language and aspirations of *The People's Rights*, Churchill's vision of a just and tolerant society is eloquently proclaimed. War and social upheaval shattered many hopes. But Churchill clung to his pre-war ideal of ameliorative reform without revolution. Those who seek to understand why he left the Liberal Party and returned to the Conservative fold in the 1920's must look back beyond the age of Bolshevik revolution and terror to the years before 1914. By associating himself with a transformed Conservative Party, Churchill was not lightly abandoning the cherished principles of his Liberal years. He was, with deep sadness, recognizing the existence of a new world.

CAMERON HAZLEHURST

CONTENTS

PREFACE

A great many people have written to ask me to publish the series of speeches which I lately delivered in Lancashire, in a form which would render them accessible to the electors. However extensive the field of political controversy may be, however varied may be the surveys we may make of it, it is inevitable that the most important subjects should be referred to on almost every occasion when one faces a great public audience. Every meeting expects to hear a clear statement upon the Lords, the Land, the Budget, and Free Trade; and, therefore, a series of speeches, if published as speeches, although they might differ in form and argument from one another, would necessarily follow to a very great extent the same path. But what suits an audience does not suit the reader. He does not care to tread a measured round half-a-dozen times over. His inclination is to dispose of one subject completely at a time, and then pass on to the next. In the arrangement of this volume I have endeavoured to suit the reader's taste. Instead of printing separate speeches, I have collected all the different references to each subject into a chapter by itself, and I have tried, so far as possible, to preserve a sense of continuity, while, at the same time, leaving each paragraph autonomous and independent. Where necessary for the completeness of the subject, I have drawn upon my earlier speeches of the present year, which have already been published in *Liberalism and the Social Problem*.

I hope that this book may serve at this juncture as a guide for some and as an armoury for others. It states, I think, some of the main arguments upon which we may rely in forms which I hope will make them simple and plain. It also outlines once again the constructive policy which has now been brought definitely into view and hangs in the balance at this fateful hour. Such as it is I offer it to my friends in the country, as ammunition passed along the firing line.

WINSTON S. CHURCHILL

BOARD OF TRADE,
   December 29th, 1909

THE PEOPLE'S RIGHTS

1 THE PEOPLE'S RIGHTS

The Quarrel. The quarrel between a tremendous democratic electorate and a one-sided hereditary chamber of wealthy men has often been threatened, has often been averted, has been long debated, has been long delayed, but it has always been inevitable, and it has come at last. It is now open, it is now flagrant, and it must now be carried to a conclusion. That quarrel arises from two events. First of all, the general election of 1906, and, secondly, the rejection session after session of the principal measures of the Government and the House of Commons then returned to power. Either of these events would have been memorable and important in itself, but taken together, placed in juxtaposition, their significance is multiplied. The election of 1906 was the most vehement expression of liberal and radical feeling that this country has ever known, and it resulted in the largest Liberal majority, both in votes and seats, of which in our lifetime, at any rate, there is any record. That election, that decision of the nation, so explicitly pronounced, was encountered directly and squarely by the most uncompromising and arbitrary assertion of aristocratic privilege upon record.

Consider what a general election is. First of all, the candidates on both sides have been in many cases for years connected with their constituencies. They have done years and months and weeks of strenuous work. They present themselves to the electors. For two or three weeks they spend their whole time in discussing and arguing political questions with masses of their fellow men. Then at last the polling day arrives. The votes are counted with scrupulous care. They are all added up, and as the result of this tremendous process — the only process of government in which you have the slightest share — 670 members, representing over six millions of electors, and a great many more who bring their influence to bear, directly and indirectly, and have to be consulted in the great decision, assemble at Westminster as a House of Commons.

There are a great many people who go about nowadays sneering at a general election. It is the fashion on the Conservative side to represent a general election as a decision which is taken on some small point of prejudice or of passing interest. We are told, for instance, that the last election was fought on the subject of Chinese labour. That was only the smallest incident in that great public decision. Of course it is quite true when public matters have to be argued out before millions of people by thousands of speakers under a party system, there will be an admixture of error and prejudice in many of the arguments that are used. But when you have made all allowance for error and prejudice and partisanship, I am bound to say that the verdict of the whole of this great United Kingdom at a general election seems to me to be the pronouncement of an august tribunal, whose approbation I most earnestly desire and from whose censures I should experience a real and genuine feeling of regret and disquietude.

The House of Lords has disdainfully swept out of existence the work of session after session. The House of Commons, called into being by the general election, meets together, months are spent in the discussion of measures and in the discussion of the details of financial administration. Practically the whole session of 1906 was devoted to the discussion

of the Education Bill, practically the whole of the session of
1908 was devoted to the discussion of the Licensing Bill, and
practically the whole of this session, the longest and the
most arduous session on record, has been devoted to the
discussion of the Budget. Now, think for one moment of
the enormous consumption of energy and knowledge and
life which this great process of election, and which this
long process of Parliamentary discussion represent and
entail — and remember that Parliamentary services in the
House of Commons are given by men who must not be
merely regarded as individuals, but who are the representatives of great constituencies, each of which has ten thousand
or twelve thousand voters, with which constituencies they
are in constant contact. And then, after the whole of this
process has been gone through, after all these measures have
been elaborately discussed in all the phases of Parliamentary
procedure, they go up to the House of Lords, and they are
swept out of existence with a disdainful gesture as if they
were of no consequence whatever. That is the way in which
the main work of three years out of the four we have been in
power has been treated by the House of Lords.

**Who are the men who claim to possess this astonishing right
to superior jurisdiction over their fellows?** What is the nature
of this assembly, which claims to use this tremendous power?
Who are these men who assert that they possess this inherent right to superior jurisdiction over their fellows? What is
the assembly which claims to exercise those astonishing
powers, and which claims to exercise them over all elective
processes and over all representative persons? What quali-
fications have they got? What are their characteristics?
What is their authority? What special knowledge do they
possess? How are they chosen? Whom do they represent? To
whom are they responsible? By whom can their action be

called in question? These are the questions which immediately arise, and these are the questions to which they have forced the mind of every thinking man in England to turn. Why should five hundred or six hundred titled persons govern us, and why should their children govern our children for ever? I invite a reply from the apologists and the admirers of the House of Lords. I invite them to show any ground of reason, or of logic, or of expediency or practical common sense in defence of the institution which has taken the predominant part during the last few days in the politics of our country.

A lingering relic of a feudal order. There is no defence, and there is no answer, except that the House of Lords — the unreformed House of Lords — has survived out of the past. It is a lingering relic of a feudal order. It is the remains, the solitary remainder of a state of things and of a balance of forces which has wholly passed away. I challenge the defenders, the backers, and the instigators of the House of Lords — I challenge them to justify and defend before the electors of the country the character and composition of the hereditary assembly.

The House of Lords has invaded the prerogative of the Crown and the rights of the Commons. Of course, as long as the House of Lords accepted a secondary and subordinate position these questions slumbered. There were other matters of great importance on which the minds of reformers were centred, and the question of altering the character of the Second Chamber and of restricting its veto, although always recognized as one of great importance, had not received that priority of consideration which in future it absolutely requires. But now that the House of Lords has grasped at the main power in the State, now that it has invaded at one

moment the prerogative of the Crown and the rights of the
House of Commons — these questions which I have put,
these fundamental questions, simple and plain, which any
man can understand, and which few can refuse to answer in
one sense, must be asked all over the country, and, being
asked, they must be answered. The answers to these questions will, I think, be fatal to the veto and to the character
of the hereditary House of Lords.

**The British monarchy has no interests divergent from those
of the British people.** There is no difficulty in vindicating the
principle of a hereditary monarchy. The experience of every
country and of all ages, the practical reasonings of common
sense, arguments of the highest theory, arguments of most
commonplace convenience, all unite to show the wisdom
which places the supreme leadership of the State beyond the
reach of private ambition and above the shocks and changes
of party strife. Further, let it not be forgotten that the
English monarchy is a limited and a constitutional monarchy. The sovereign reigns but he does not govern — that
is a maxim which we were all taught out of our school books.
The powers of government are exercised upon the advice of
Ministers responsible to Parliament, and those Ministers are
capable of being displaced, and are very frequently displaced,
by the House of Commons freely elected by millions of
electors. The British monarchy has no interests divergent
from those of the British people.

It is based on the abiding and prevailing interests of the nation.
It enshrines only those ideas and causes upon which the
whole British people are united. It is based on the abiding
and prevailing interests of the nation, and thus, through all
the changes of the last hundred years, through all the wide
developments of the democratic State, the English monarchy

has become the most secure, as it is the most ancient and glorious, monarchy in the whole of Christendom. It is important to draw these great distinctions at the outset of a controversy which, although at present confined to the restriction of the Lords' veto, must inevitably raise the whole question of a hereditary second chamber.

The House of Lords are refusing supplies to the Crown. The House of Lords, in rejecting the Budget which provides for the national expenditure of the year, are refusing, for the first time since the great Rebellion, aids and supplies to the Crown, and by that fact and by their intrusion upon finance they commit an act of violence against the British Constitution. There is no precedent of any kind for the rejection of a Budget Bill by the House of Lords in all the long annals of the British Parliament, or, before that, in the still more venerable annals of the English Parliament. The custom of centuries forbids their intrusion upon finance. The opinions and the judgments of all their most famous statesmen, all the great men who have led the Tory Party, concur in recognizing the sanctity of that custom. Lord Chatham, Mr Pitt, the Duke of Wellington, and the late Lord Salisbury all may be cited as declaring in unequivocal terms that the House of Lords have no right to interfere with money Bills. Those pronouncements even increase in definiteness as they become more modern. The latest declaration is the most emphatic. Only a year ago, almost to the month, Mr Balfour, the leader of the Opposition, spoke at Dumfries and used these words — I wonder what he thinks of them today: —'It is the House of Commons, and not the House of Lords, which settles uncontrolled our financial system.' The very language of the King's Speech, the very preamble of the Budget Bill itself, referring as they do upon finance particularly to the House of Commons alone, show how deeply this maxim has sunk into our constitutional life. Every text-book ever written on the British Constitution, every history ever compiled of the English people has the same confirmatory declaration to make. Now we are told that the whole constitutional principle is to be repudiated and trampled upon; and by whom?

The Conservative Party should have respected constitutional usage. One would have thought that the Conservative Party, who vaunt themselves as the party of law and order, of loyalty to the Constitution, and respect for ancient and venerable usage, would have bowed to the force of facts and arguments like these. After all, the Constitution has served them well. Even under the democratic franchise of 1885 they have enjoyed seventeen years of power as against seven in which power has been exercised by their opponents. One would at any rate have thought that the House of Lords, whose existence in its present form finds absolutely no justification except in the grey yet not inglorious past of British institutions, would have been specially careful of old acceptances and would have set the example, even when it did not suit their personal interests, of bowing to old observances. But no! At the first moment when there is a chance, as they think, of scoring a point in the party game, of striking at an administration which they dislike, of securing an immunity for themselves from particular forms of taxation, the whole majestic fabric of custom and observance, of precedent and of law, is to be chucked cynically overboard, and upon the calculations of the party caucus, under pressure of the rich men's Press, and above all upon the sinister compulsion of the drink traffic, the House of Lords has determined, so we are assured, deliberately to plunge into a course of reckless and undisguised opportunism.

Why the Commons must control finance. 1. The control of finance means the control of the whole administration of the country. You must realize fully the significance of finance. Upon finance in a civilized nation everything connected with government turns. If the Government control the money-bags they control the whole administration of the country. The House that has the power of the purse must be the source and origin of political power. For hundreds of years that power has resided in the House of Commons — that is to say it has resided in the assembly which is elected, which if you do not like you can change, and whose members are amenable to your control and have to come before you to solicit your votes. Now it is suggested that that power is also to be exercised by the House of Lords. I submit to you that it is quite impossible to have two chambers in one country both exercising the power of the purse unless they are both elected and both swing together with the general view of the electors.

2. If the Lords exercise that control the Constitution becomes unworkable. Otherwise you will certainly have the executive Government of the day ordering the ships, engaging the soldiers, embarking on the expenditure of these administrative projects, making its plans for raising money to pay for all these things at the beginning of the year, and six months afterwards, when the Bill has gone through the House of Commons, these lordly persons, who know nothing at all about finance, to whom no estimates are submitted, who have not the right to alter or vary a single tax, who cannot fix the expenditure and cannot alter an item in that expenditure or increase it in any way — these people, to whom no statement of the financial position is made, now claim the right to intervene, even in November, and send the whole financial system in the country head over heels, and say they will send the House of Commons back to the constituencies. You may have a political system that is good or bad, that is Conservative or Liberal, but that is an impossible system judged by every standard and by all kinds of conditions. And so much is it an impossible system that we have come to the conclusion that we shall not continue to bear the burdens and responsibilities of office unless we are given by the British people full and effective powers to discharge those responsibilities.

Has the House of Lords ever done right in any of the great controversies of the last 100 years? What is the record of the House of Lords in modern times? How have they used the great power which they claim? It is a big question which I am going to ask you. Have they ever been right in any of the great controversies of the last 100 years? Were they right in refusing for so long religious emancipation for the Roman Catholics? Were they right in resisting the removal of Jewish disabilities? Were they right in denying to the dissenters access to the universities? Were they right in resisting, till they almost drove the country into revolution and civil war, the passage of the great Reform Bill? Were they well advised in opposing the House of Commons in the repeated efforts which it made to secure the purity of its own elections? Were they right in resisting the Ballot Bill, which alone can secure to the humble voter the assurance that he can cast his franchise which the State accords him without prejudice to his personal interest? Were they right in resisting the abolition of purchase in the Army — that memorable reform of Mr Cardwell, the last great Liberal War Minister before Mr Haldane — that great reform which, as it was well said at the time, was designed to take the Army out of pawn? There is not a single one of these controversies not now definitely settled. Nobody disputes, nobody questions for a moment, that in every one of these cases the settlement at which we have arrived is the right one. In every case that settlement had been previously resisted by the Lords.

In every one of these controversies which have passed away altogether from the area of dispute, and about which all the men of all the parties are agreed, the House of Lords has been proved to be absolutely wrong.

The Lords and the settlement in South Africa. It is very likely that we could not have made our settlement in South Africa, which everyone today admits to have been crowned by brilliant and immeasurable success, unless by a lucky accident, which I admit filled me with astonishment when I was at the Colonial Office, it had been possible to give these great Constitutions to the Transvaal and the Orange Free State by Letters Patent under the Crown without the need of bringing them before the House of Lords. Certain I am that if we had had to submit these Constitutions, which were framed with great care by the executive Government and approved by the House of Commons, to the House of Lords, to the judgment of such a Peer, such an evil counsellor as Lord Milner, they would have been so mutilated and so mauled that they would not have been accepted by South Africa. They would not have healed the wounds, they would not have won the hearts, they would not have gained for Britain in the years that are to come the loyal support and co-operation of one of the strongest and most valiant races of the world.

The partisan arbitration of the House of Lords. I want to ask on what principle does the House of Lords deal with the legislation it receives from the House of Commons. Does it act impartially? Is it a Chamber of review and restraint? Do the Lords, for instance, reject Bills which are extreme, and pass Bills which are moderate in their character? Is that the standard by which they judge? Do they act according to their judgment and conscience? Not one of these questions can be answered in the affirmative by any man who honestly and quietly asks them of himself. Again I say without hesitation that the attitude of the Lords towards all the measures which reach them from the House of Commons is entirely partisan. I say that they pass Bills which they believe to be wrong, when they think it will pay the Tories to have the question settled, and they reject Bills, however moderate they may be, however pervaded by the spirit of compromise and conciliation, when they think they will injure the Liberal Party by keeping the question open. That is the sole canon by which the House of Lords — this Second Chamber which we are exhorted to believe has the supreme monopoly of political wisdom — that is the sole canon, the canon of caucus, that is the sole test by which they judge of the legislation they receive.

The Education Act of 1906. Take the Education Act of 1906 — if there was any fault in that Act, it was that we had gone too far in the direction of compromise, Still, on its third reading, as the result of the concession the Government offered in the final form in which it left the House of Commons, the Education Act received the support of the Irish Roman Catholics in the House of Commons, and went from the House of Commons with the largest majority, I think, ever behind an Education Bill. The late Duke of Devonshire, a man of middle mind, just impartiality, and disinterested integrity, said in his place in the House of Lords that on the whole he thought the Bill ought to pass into law in order to set the long controversy at rest. Therefore, he told the House of Lords they ought to pass the Bill. But they rejected it. Why? Because they knew perfectly well that so long as this question remained unsettled it would be an injury and a cause of division to their Liberal opponents.

The Licensing Act of 1908. It would be a great thing for the country to have the drink question settled. If there is one matter which the people of this country might have expected the Lords to allow the people to settle for themselves, you would think it would be the conditions upon which the sale of intoxicating drink should be sold in their own neighbourhoods. Each district has to pay for the expense of disease, crime, misery, and destitution which follows from the excessive use of alcohol. If there is any question you would have expected these fortunate and lucky Peers, wealthy men, with all their advantages of education and easy outlook upon life; if there is any subject upon which you would expect them to allow the nation to take the lead, it is on the question of temperance. And yet on purely tactical grounds — because it was important to the Conservative Party to keep the public-house vote — in spite of the advice of the middle-minded men, in spite of the appeals of the Bishops of the Church — to their honour — and the Archbishop of Canterbury, the House of Lords cast away this Bill upon which the whole labour of the House of Commons had been spent; and by that act sent a message of despair to every social worker, to every philanthropic body, to every Christian minister, and to every little Sunday school throughout the land.

The Trades Disputes Act. Those are the Bills they rejected. Let me now speak of two Bills they have passed. The Trades Disputes Act — a Bill which has my entire sympathy and agreement — that Bill was described by Lord Halsbury as an outrageous and tyrannous Bill, a section of which was more disgraceful than could be found in any statute. The strongest

opinions were expressed against that Bill, and I think it is
not unfair to the House of Lords to say that the vast majority of its members regarded it as a vicious and immoral
measure. But they passed it. And why did they pass it?
They passed it because they thought it would not suit the
Tory Party for the House of Lords to run up against the
great Trade Unions by rejecting the Bill.

The Old-Age Pensions Act. And then I come to the Old-Age
Pensions. The House of Lords have passed the Old-Age
Pensions Act, and I see that Lord Lansdowne takes credit
for having passed it. He said — I will read you his words —
'We did not desire to stand in the way of the measure, and
we allowed it to become law.' Thank you so much. But what
did he say while the Bill was passing through the House of
Lords? This is what Lord Lansdowne said about this measure for which he now takes credit: 'A measure', he said,
'which we regard with great apprehension, and which we
fear may have very far-reaching effects upon the future of
this country.' Again: 'This measure, I am afraid, is one
which will weaken the moral fibre of the nation, and diminish the self-respect of our people.' You will observe that, in
Lord Lansdowne's opinion, the work-house was the only
method by which the self-respect of our people could be
maintained; but, although Lord Lansdowne took such strong
action about the Old-Age Pensions Act, although his friends
and supporters used even stronger language than he, they
passed it, although they thought it would demoralize the
country and sap the self-respect of our nation — they passed
it. They thought that it was not good ground to fight upon.

**The House of Lords has 'allowed' the Liberal Government to
govern the country for four years.** It is indisputable that the
use of the veto of the Peers during the present Parliament has

been dictated by party feeling, by party interest, and not by any regard to the merits of the Bill or the interests, as they conceive them, of the country. Lord Lansdowne says of the Old-Age Pensions Act, 'We allowed it to pass.' Note that phrase, because it reveals his whole attitude of mind and the attitude of those whom he leads in the House of Lords — that is to say, nine-tenths of the assembly. More: 'We have allowed a lot of other Bills to pass too.' And he boasts of them to the select Liberal Unionists gathered in council at Plymouth — 'the Port of London Bill we have allowed to pass; the Labour Exchanges Act, we have allowed that to pass; the Trade Boards Bill to deal with sweating; the Small Holdings Bill; and the Housing and Town Planning Bill, we have let all these pass.' We have conceded all these to you — to you, you miserable members of the House of Commons. And yet you are not grateful. But more: we have allowed the Liberal Government to govern the country for four years. We have actually passed all their Budgets except this one. We have permitted them to pass. We have been graciously pleased, of our lordly wisdom and generosity, to extend to them our tolerance, and have allowed Ministers opposed to us in politics to hold the offices bestowed on them by the authority of the Crown and the support of the nation. And then the Radicals complain. Then they are not satisfied. Then they talk of the arbitrary interference of the Peers!

The astonishing moderation of the House of Lords. How unreasonable, that we should go about complaining against them. 'Why,' say the House of Lords, 'we might have thrown out every Bill' — it is quite true, they might — 'but we did not do it. We allowed you to pass those Bills which we did not think would cost us any inconvenience or damage to our party interest. We might have rejected every Budget, we might have disordered the finances every year, but we

B

did not do it. We might have sent the House of Commons packing back to the constituencies every autumn before we went off to Scotland for the grouse. We have not done it. For four whole years we have actually allowed representative Government to continue unchallenged and untouched.' That is the point of view. The House of Lords stands at the present moment, like Lord Clive, astonished at its own moderation.

The reasons for rejecting the Budget refuted. I come to the rejection of the Budget, that memorable event in English history of which all the little boys in the schools a hundred years hence will read. What are Lord Lansdowne's reasons advanced in justification of that act? I take the three principal reasons from his speech at Plymouth: (1) The Government 'have created a colossal deficit.' (2) They have 'raided the Sinking Fund.' (3) The finance of the Budget has 'created a panic destructive of confidence and credit, in consequence of which unemployment has come into our midst.' These are the words I copied down from the report of his speech. Now look at these three reasons.

1. The Budget has *not* created a panic—trade is reviving. Take the last one first. Lord Lansdowne's assertion that the Budget created a panic destructive of confidence and credit, in consequence of which unemployment came into our midst, is absolutely untrue. I say there are no facts whatever to sustain it. On the contrary, there are innumerable facts to disprove it. The business of the Stock Exchange of London — the great heart of the nation, from the House of Lords point of view — the Stock Exchange has been exceptionally active. The value of the 387 representative securities is more today than it was on the day before the Chancellor of the Exchequer unfolded his Budget proposals. Trade is reviving.

There is an increasing export of manufactured articles, and an increasing import of raw material — a sure sign of increasing exports in the future. Employment is better every month since Mr Lloyd George's Budget was introduced, and it has got better every month in spite of a seasonal tendency the other way, because it is worse in winter than in summer. In the month of October unemployment was twenty-five per cent better than in the same month last year. Well, what are you to think of a man — I beg pardon — what are you to think of an irremovable marquis and a permanent and heaven-born legislator who founds the whole of his argument when he is publicly submitting his case at this crisis to the country on a total and absolute mis-statement and perversion of a simple notorious fact?

2. The Government has repaid debt while other countries are meeting expenditure by loans. What is the second charge — that he was justified in rejecting the Budget, because we had 'raided the Sinking Fund'? I rubbed my eyes when I read that. What is our record, and what is their record in the payment of debt? The Government of which Lord Lansdowne was a member was the Government that made the South African war, that muddled through the South African war, that added 150 millions to the capital indebtedness of this country, and even after the war was over, the only provision which they made for the repayment of debt was so ineffective that scarcely two millions or, at the outside, three millions, of the increased war debt were paid off in their time. We came into power, and under the management of the Exchequer by Mr Asquith we had paid off nearly one-third of the whole extra burden which they placed upon the finances by the South African war. That is a provision for the repayment of debt without example in time of peace, except for the purpose of paying a war indemnity, in any great State which I can recollect; and even at this moment, when we are confronted with so many demands for expenditure, we are paying off debt, reducing the aggregate capital liabilities of the State by nearly seven millions a year, whilst every other country in the world almost — in Europe certainly — is paying its ordinary expenditure out of loans. Well, a man — or a marquis — must be pretty hard up for an argument when at a crisis like this he has to accuse the present Government with its unexampled austerity in the repayment of debt, with having raided the Sinking Fund.

3. The deficit is for Old-Age Pensions and the Navy. And what is his third charge? It is that we have created a colossal deficit. What item of that deficit does he challenge? Old-Age Pensions? Why, it was only a moment ago that he was taking credit for having allowed that Bill to pass into law. If you allow Pensions to pass into law, I suppose you ought to allow the legislation which is to pay for them to pass into law too. Who promised Old-Age Pensions? Who hawked them about at three elections before the eyes of the people? When the Pensions Act was passed through the House of Commons did not the Tories move amendments, supported by their official Whips, which would have raised the cost to fourteen millions? Then it is rather late in the day to turn round and accuse the Government of having created a deficit on account of Old-Age Pensions when they as a party promised them first, and when they did everything in their power to increase — recklessly increase — the expenses necessary for that purpose. Then the Navy. That is the second great item which has created the deficit. What is the good of Lord Lansdowne challenging our action in creating that deficit? Why, Lord Lansdowne and the party he represents have been doing all they can to raise up an odious and artificial scare which would enormously swell the expenses. What right of reproach have they against us?

Mr Balfour and the limitation of the Lords' powers. No, the House of Lords has no right to reject the Budget. Custom, procedure, and authority are against them. All the great minds of the past, all the moderate and impartial men of the present — no one has spoken more strongly against the rights of the House of Lords to touch money Bills than Mr Balfour. Everyone is familiar with his words. They cannot be too widely circulated at this election. I think they will go far to render his advocacy useless during the next few weeks. It is quite clear that he is defending the action of the House of Lords which a year ago, or two or three years ago, he deliberately stigmatized as unconstitutional and beyond their power.

The House of Lords claims to tinker, tamper, and meddle with every kind of legislation. The whole movement of the world is against the intrusion of the House of Lords upon legislation. As democracy becomes more numerous and educated, more varied, more complex, and more powerful, it is necessary that the House of Lords should recede and retire. It is necessary that it should count less and less. Most men expected that gradually, as things happen in the history of our country, the House of Lords would pass peacefully and painlessly away. That would have been a natural evolution — much better for us, and much better for them. But what do you see? On the contrary, the House of Lords put their claims higher every year. They now claim to reject every Bill, no matter by what majority it is supported in the House of Commons, or how newly elected that house is. They claim to tinker, tamper, and meddle with every kind of subject, many of which they very imperfectly understand.

They have mutilated the principal legislation of this Parliament until at last a climax has been reached, and by a violent act the executive Government has been brought to a standstill; and so we come to a dissolution, in which the House of Lords comes face to face with the electors in a fierce collision which must involve a constitutional change.

The absolute breakdown of the Constitution. The control of finance is the root of all civilized government. The whole plan of the executive and the administration depends upon finance. The power of finance cannot be exercised by two Chambers, unless those two Chambers act together in general unity. And you are brought to this clear alternative. Finance must be given wholly to one Chamber, as it has been in the past, or else both Chambers must be elected simultaneously. That alternative is brought about by the absolute breakdown of the Constitution and the administrative machinery. That is why we as a Government will not be willing to discharge the responsibilities of Government, whatever our majority, under the state of things which the action of the House of Lords has created.

It is of real advantage that there should be two great parties. Is it not of real advantage to the country that there should be two great parties each capable in turn of providing responsible administrations for the service of the Crown? Does not that fact, that men of both parties and millions of working men have a chance from time to time to help to choose the Government — does not that associate the whole body of the nation in one way or another in the high duties and with the glorious inheritance of the British Empire? How much better our system of Government has worked upon this balance than in those countries where there is a permanent governing class, with all the interests of wealth and privilege massed around them keeping the rest of their fellow countrymen in sullen subjection by force of arms. That is the position of more than one European country today. A powerful Imperialist and militarist combination holding all the power and confronting a vast Socialist Party utterly estranged from the fundamental institutions of the State. That is a condition which everyone who cares about the future of our country and who understands the story of this famous island would labour and would struggle to save us from. But that is an inevitable result of the change in the Constitution which the House of Lords has now attempted.

If every Liberal Government could only hold office by favour of their bitter foes, the House of Lords, brute force and class hatred would become the characteristics of British political life. If no Liberal Government were able to pass any measures except those which commend themselves to a permanent majority of their political opponents — if every Liberal Government could only hold office from year to year by the favour and upon the sufferance of their bitter foes in the House of Lords, if at any moment, upon some pretext or other, a Liberal Government was liable to have the whole structure of the nation's finance brought clattering about their ears, then it is certain that the reign of two great parties, differing widely, no doubt, in conviction, in sentiment, in character and motive, but united in a common loyalty to the Crown and Empire, has closed for ever, and we shall be face to face with a period when parties would necessarily be grouped upon violent and revolutionary lines, and when brute force and class hatred, instead of forbearance and public spirit, will become the characteristics of British political life. It is from these perils that we rely upon the genius and sagacity of the British electors to preserve, at this juncture, the foundations of the State.

The people's account with the Lords is a long and heavy one.
Our account with the Lords is long and heavy. We decline
to judge the House of Lords only by their action upon the
Budget. We remember the ill-usage and humiliation that the
great majority which returned Sir Henry Campbell-Banner-
man to power suffered during its first three years of office.
The House of Lords must be judged by their character and
conduct as a whole. We have seen them claim to veto or
destroy, even without discussion, any legislation, however
important, sent to them by any majority, however large,
from any House of Commons, however newly elected. We
have seen them use these unconscionable rights in party
interests, in class interests, and in personal interests. We
have seen them use the power they should not hold at all,
which, if they hold at all, they should hold in trust for all, to
play a violent, calculated, aggressive party game.

We have seen an immense majority returned after the
labours of an election to support the Liberal administration,
and we have seen the legislation of that Government thrown
out in the most arbitrary fashion year after year.

Now at last, as the climax of all these intolerable proceed-
ings, we have seen them reject the Budget.

**The House of Lords is responsible to no one; it represents no
one.** In a free country all public institutions and public
functionaries have a regulated action. The Crown acts on the
advice of Ministers, Ministers are subject to the day-to-day
control of the Commons; the House of Commons is elected
by millions of the people.

Everyone is responsible to someone. The high officers of
State, the great governors and generals and admirals are
removable by the executive Government. Even the judges
can be displaced upon a joint address by both Houses of
Parliament. Nobody, however powerful, in our country,

nobody, however venerated, no office, however august, but in a free nation there are checks and controls surrounding them. The House of Lords constitutes a single and solitary exception in the whole of this tremendous chain of interdependent responsibility and obligation. It accepts no advice, except what it chooses to take from the Tory caucus. It is responsible to no one; it represents no one. The Lords exercise their own sweet will at their own sweet pleasure and discretion, and they now claim uncontrolled and unreformed — mind that, unreformed — to seize and hold the main power in the government of the whole country. Such a claim cannot be admitted. It will be repudiated by every man of spirit. We reject their pretensions. We deny their competence, and we ask you to enable us to take the necessary steps to punish their intrusion.

The Lords' plan of 'Heads I win: tails you don't get paid'. You will be told the Lords only seek to learn the will of the people. They who fought against reform and the extension of the franchise till this country was nearly rocketed into revolution; they who continued to resist every extension of the franchise, now come forward posing as the true apostles of democracy. He is a very simple fellow who lets himself be taken in by that. The Lords seek to escape the Budget and to destroy the Government, not to ascertain the true will of the people. And they think they can embark upon this course of adventure on a very curious plan. I will tell you their plan. 'Heads I win: tails you don't get paid.' If (so they argue) the electors return a majority to support the House of Lords then the Lords' position will be enormously strengthened; then the House of Commons will be reduced to a subservient place in the Constitution, the Tory Government will be reinstated in power, and taxes will be raised on bread and meat instead of on incomes and land values, and

they will be spent on armaments and jingo policies instead
of upon social reform, and everything in the garden will be
absolutely grand. But if, on the other hand, the electors vote
against the Lords, then, we are told, Oh, the Lords will pass
the Budget, and they will wait till the end of the year before
they make up their mind whether they will throw out the
next. That is their view of what will happen. And when I
study their newspaper and read their speeches, and familiar-
ize myself with their mind upon this subject, I can only say
that they have got a great deal to learn in the next few weeks.

**Counterchecks upon democratic assemblies must be con-
ceived in the national interest.** Counterchecks upon a democratic assembly there may be, I believe there ought to be;
but those counterchecks should be in the nature of delay and
not in the nature of arrest. They should operate equally and
evenly against both political parties and not against only
one of them. Above all they should be counterchecks
conceived in the national interest and not in a partisan interest. The abuses and absurdities connected with the House
of Lords have now reached a point when the effective restriction of their veto not only upon finance but upon legislation
has become the dominant issue of a memorable election.

**The Lords have rejected the Budget out of their love for the
working classes.** There are some people — I daresay I may be
one of them — who have been going about the country saying
that the House of Lords have rejected the Budget because
they did not like it. But we are assured this is not true. If
they have violated the Constitution, if they have insulted
the rights of the House of Commons and trespassed upon the
prerogative of the Crown, and if they have refused and intercepted the supplies demanded by the sovereign, they have
not done it on their own account; they have only done it

out of their love for the working classes, out of their sincere respect for public opinion, out of their affection for democratic processes and the processes of popular election. It is true, no doubt, that they have not shown these desires so markedly before. They have in the past resisted every grant and every extension of the franchise. They have resisted every attempt to reform the machinery of popular election, and when the Conservatives were in power—during the whole seventeen years the Conservatives were in power— the House of Lords exhibited no desire to learn the will of the people.

When did the Lords want to learn the will of the people? No, they never even wanted to learn the will of the people before the country was plunged into the South African war. They never asked the will of the people before the majority given to a Conservative Government for the express purpose of finishing the South African war was used for a Licensing Bill and an Education Bill to which great numbers who had voted for that Government were fundamentally opposed. They never asked the will of the people during the last two years of Mr Balfour's administration, years which were a scandal and an offence upon representative government. But all of you know how suddenly sometimes conversion comes to a man. The light flashes in his eyes, and his soul is melted within him; and we see the House of Lords at this moment consumed with a passionate and burning desire to ascertain the will of the people, and to embrace the heaving bosom of democracy. Nothing will hold them back. Nothing will restrain them. No consideration of prudence, no consideration of patriotism, no consideration of tradition, and of the usages of the Constitution, to which alone the House of Lords owe their continued existence. No, nothing will restrain them. They must come forward into the field of democracy and appeal to the people — and I really think we shall have to oblige them.

The Lords do not think of themselves — they cannot bear to see the working man's tobacco and whisky taxed! There are others who go about the country saying — and again I may be one of them — who go about the country saying that the Lords don't like the Budget because of the taxes upon high incomes, upon great estates, upon liquor licences, and upon land values. But we are informed that that is a Radical calumny. They have never thought of themselves in all this business. It is not these taxes which they mind at all. Oh, no; they do not mind these in the least. What they cannot bear, is to see the tobacco of the working man taxed by a Liberal Government. That is what upsets Lord Revelstoke. That is what disturbs the Duke of Northumberland. Then they cannot bear to see the whisky which cheers the humble homes of the people until there is very often very little home left to cheer — they cannot bear to see the whisky — 'that liquid food', as it has been described — so cruelly reduced in consumption, that a marked and sensible difference is being made in the habits of the people. That is what breaks Lord Lansdowne's honest heart.

The food taxes are to unite the Empire. Others again say, and this is, we are assured, another Radical extravagance, that the House of Lords hope, in the hurly-burly, to establish a Protective tariff to enable them to charge higher prices for the corn and meat produced on their landed estates and to enable them to shift a portion of direct taxation on to the shoulders of the indirect taxpayer. That is another wicked calumny. It is quite true that this would and must inevitably follow as a result of the proposals of the House of Lords and the Conservative Party. It is inevitable that as the result of the taxes on bread and on meat, and of the great increase of indirect taxation which would accompany these taxes, both the consequences to which I have referred would necessarily follow. But that is not the motive of the House of Lords. They have not been thinking of this. Oh no! Their motive in wanting to put taxes on corn is to unite our great and glorious Empire by the sacred bonds of food taxation. Their desire to levy import duties on foreign goods is not to relieve themselves of any burden, but to make more work for the working man. Ah!

The public-spirited offer of the Lords to take over the whole business of governing the country. You must remember that the House of Lords have very lately made us a public-spirited offer of the highest importance. They have offered to take over the whole business of governing the country. They have offered to save us all the trouble and worry and vexation and anxiety of governing ourselves. The only thing they do not offer to take over is the expense. But everything else is to be done for us. We put the penny in the slot; they do the rest. There is a great deal of disturbance and labour and friction caused by the election of members of Parliament. It costs the country a lot of money; it is very disturbing to trade; it excites a lot of people by making them feel that they have a right to take part in the government of their land. And what is it all for, if when the members return to Westminster all their work, session after session, is to be swept away and cast upon the rubbish heap? Why, the question arises in the breasts of the House of Lords, would it not be very much better to make a good job of it, and let the Peers have the control not merely over legislation, but over finance as well? Why, then we could enjoy the services in government of Lord Milner, fresh from his great work of peace and reconciliation in South Africa; and we could enjoy the services of Lord Curzon, who is much too important a man, as I am sure you will agree, to demean himself by standing for the House of Commons and mixing himself up with you and me and a lot of other common people, but who, if the House of Lords were entrusted with the supreme power in the State, would be quite ready to govern us from his position in the House of Lords just as he governed for some years the mild Hindu. And if any of these distinguished pro-consular administrators were to get wearied of the burden of State, there are 400 or 500 backwoodsmen Peers, all meditating on their estates on the great questions of Government, all studying *Ruff's Guide* and other blue books, all revolving the problems of Empire and of Epsom, everyone of them a heaven-born, God-granted legislator, who knows by instinct what the people want, every one of them with a stake in the heart of the country, all ready to come forward and fill the gap, if Lord Milner or Lord Curzon should flag. Now, I think this is a very bold bid, and a very bold offer. Let us consider it well. The hammer is about to fall on the bargain, and the fact that this offer has been made fully justifies us in giving them some testimonial that will last, and that will show them that we fully appreciate what they have done, and what they would like to do.

The pretensions of the Lords. The House of Lords have only been tolerated all these years because they were thought to be in a comatose condition which preceded dissolution. They have got to dissolution now. That this body, utterly unrepresentative, utterly unreformed, should come forward and claim the right to make and unmake Governments, should lay one greedy paw on the prerogative of the sovereign and another upon the long-established and most fundamental privileges of the House of Commons is a spectacle which a year ago no one would have believed could happen; which fifty years ago no Peer would have dared to suggest; and which two hundred years ago would not have been discussed in the amiable though active manner of a political campaign, but would have been settled by charges of cavalry and the steady advance of iron-clad pikemen.

But although methods change, causes remain and forces remain; and that is what they are going to learn.

Is self-government to be taken out of our hands? This is a very large and complex community, and we have been under the impression that we governed ourselves. Six or seven million people have votes, and the wealthier and more educated members of the community have an immense influence over a great number of the poorer citizens; and the community has felt itself in the enjoyment of full powers of self-government. We have created great industries, we have given self-government to powerful States, we have scattered free Parliaments all over the world, and taught the rest of the world the advantages of representative institutions. In Russia, in Turkey, in Persia, wherever an attempt is made, however crude, however primitive, to give the nation a share in its own government, it is to this island, to this nation, that all eyes are turned. Are we really going, at the beginning of the twentieth century, to have our self-government taken out of our hands and put into the power of a knot of perfectly ordinary, unrepresentative, and highly prejudiced persons who claim the right to rule us by divine authority; who claim the right to say — in their lordly wisdom, amenable to no one, permanent, irremovable, beyond the reach of any protest that we can make — to say what is good for us and what is not?

Are we to be tied up in the leading strings of snobbishness and antiquated usage? We are not the aboriginal inhabitants of some newly discovered South Sea islands. We are not the children who are being educated in the schools. We are the leading civilized community in the world, and we are not going to have our affairs mismanaged, and we are not going to have our national name degraded by being tied up in the leading strings of snobbishness and antiquated usage. The British Constitution slowly expands and moves forwards. Always from year to year we are associating new classes in the Government of the country. The waters gradually accumulate behind an obstruction. They gather and grow, and for a long time the dam holds. Then comes a great head of waters and a strong wind behind them, and the forward movement is made. This is the time for the forward movement. We have all wondered when the moment would come. We all have known it was bound to come. It has come now.

There is no class hatred in our country. There is very little class hatred in our country. Those who go about trying to appeal to class hatred very soon find themselves talking to an unresponsive audience. There is no hatred in this country of the Peer as a Peer. Far from it. He is always taken not merely upon his merits, but with an extra advantage given to him — always — and so it will be unless they set themselves up as a caste against the commonweal. It is from that danger we are going to rescue them.

Our movement carries us forward to a broader and more equal age. I believe our movement, vehement as it must become in the next few weeks, carries with it no menace to the stability of society, no menace to the security of property. The stability of society will be increased by the removal of preventable misery. The security of property will only be maintained by the establishment of just laws regulating its acquisition and by a fair distribution of public burdens. And I believe that movement carries with it no menace to the historical continuity of our English life, but, on the contrary, it is a natural and long-due step in evolution which will carry us forward to a broader consolidation of our liberties.

Lord Curzon's defence of the Peers. When I began my campaign in Lancashire I challenged any Conservative speaker to come down and say why the House of Lords, composed as the present House of Lords is, should have the right to rule over us, and why the children of that House of Lords should have the right to rule over our children. My challenge has been taken up with great courage by Lord Curzon. The House of Lords could not have found any more able and, I will add, any more arrogant defender, and at Oldham on Wednesday — you have heard of Oldham — so have I. Well, at Oldham Lord Curzon treated a great public meeting to what I can only call a prize essay on the Middle Ages. I do not say it was not a very eloquent speech. It was a beautiful speech. I read it with the most intense pleasure, with feelings of artistic pleasure, and also a sense of satisfaction, because I would like Lord Curzon to make that speech in every town and city throughout our country. I would ask nothing better than that he should have an opportunity of putting these views forward with all his ability and address to great audiences throughout the country. I am sure it would save some of us a lot of trouble.

The sovereign is not a hereditary legislator. Let us look at one or two of the arguments on which Lord Curzon relied. He began with a defence of hereditary legislators. That is a very plucky thing to do. He said, 'Look at the monarchy!' But the sovereign is not a hereditary legislator. In this country the sovereign reigns but he does not govern. The king acts

on the advice of Ministers. The Crown in England has not had
for hundreds of years the power of making laws, and for two
or three centuries has not had the power of stopping laws
when they have been passed by Parliament. It is as a constitutional monarchy that we reverence and honour the British
Crown. I do not think the people of England would be prepared for one moment to agree to the sovereign of these
realms exercising the power which the Tsar of Russia
exercises. Lord Curzon could scarcely have chosen a more
inappropriate instance upon which to rely.

Heredity and a representative system. Then he told us that
Pitt, Fox, and Grenville in days gone by exercised great
dominance in the House of Commons, and that forty years
later all their sons were also in great offices and playing a
very important part. He went on to say that something like
that had reproduced itself today, though on a smaller scale.
Whereas some years ago you had Mr Gladstone, Mr
Chamberlain, and Lord Robert Cecil (afterwards Lord
Salisbury) in the House of Commons, so now you saw their
sons distinguished. Then he turned to me. Did I not owe
something to my father? Why, of course, I owe everything
to my father. But what defence is all this of a House of
hereditary legislators? Because my father was member for
Woodstock, I do not suggest that I should be permanently
member for Woodstock, irrespective of what the people of
Woodstock might think of me. It is quite true that some
instances can be cited of men who have succeeded distinguished fathers and have attained equal and even greater
distinction themselves. But how many cases can be shown
of the contrary? You can almost count the hereditary instances on your fingers. But only consider the enormous
number of contrary instances which have been veiled in a
decent and merciful obscurity. If the electors of a particular

constituency like to let old associations count — if they choose
to say 'We will vote for this young man because we knew
his father' — what derogation is that from their free right
of choice; in what way is their full power to choose their own
representative affected? If the argument of Lord Curzon
proves anything, it proves that heredity will receive favour
under a representative system wherever it deserves it.

A claim to be rejected with contempt. But the claim of the
House of Lords is not, that, if the electors so decide, the sons
of distinguished men may have legislative functions entrusted to them; it is that, whether the electors like it or not,
the sons and the grandsons and the great-grandsons, and so
on till the end of time, of distinguished men shall have legislative functions entrusted to them. That claim requires that
we should maintain in our country a superior caste, with
law-giving functions inherent in their blood, transmissible by
them to their remotest posterity, and that these functions
should be exercised irrespective of the character, the intelligence, or the experience of the tenant for the time being, and
utterly independent of the public need and the public will.
That is a proposition which only needs to be stated before
any average British jury to be rejected with spontaneous
contempt. Why has it never been rejected before? In my
opinion it has never been rejected, because the House of
Lords has never before been taken seriously by the democratic electorate, which has been in existence since 1885.
They have never been taken seriously because they were
believed to be in a comatose and declining condition, upon
which death would gradually supervene. Now we see the
House of Lords stepping into the front rank of politics; not
merely using their veto over legislation, but also claiming
new powers over the whole of the finances — powers which
would make them the main governing centre in the State.

That is why we are forced to examine their pretensions very closely; and when we have examined them, I venture to think there will not be much left of them.

Peers and 'gusts of popular passion'. 'Oh, but', says Lord Curzon, going on with his defence of this hereditary Chamber, 'we don't have to trim our sails to catch passing gusts of popular passion.' Well, what are they doing now? Their whole contention is that they consider the Budget is a bad Budget, that it is wrong and vicious, and that it will do all manner of evil to the country. But they say if at the election the nation, the electors, upon a gust of popular passion, return a majority favourable to the Budget they will immediately pass the Budget. That may be very prudent of them, and it may be very proper of them, but it certainly is not standing against the gusts of popular passion. And what about the Trades Disputes Act? Why, I don't hesitate to say that the House of Lords, or a great majority of that House, regarded that as a thoroughly wicked Bill. Lord Halsbury, the ex-Lord Chancellor, described it as pernicious and wicked, as a Bill which contained a section more disgraceful than had appeared in any other statute. But it had what the House of Lords thought was 'a gust of popular passion' behind it; they stepped aside, and it passed.

Then there were the Old-Age Pensions, which were denounced by Lord Lansdowne and by many others in the House of Lords in unmeasured terms as being a system calculated to destroy thrift and to weaken the self-respect of the working classes. So great was the dislike of the Peers to the measure that they actually carried an amendment saying that after five or six years the whole system should come up again for review and would lapse if it were not renewed. But that is where 'a gust of popular passion' came in. The Bill was passed though they believed it was going to ruin the country. I am very glad it was passed. But what credentials does this conduct give the House of Lords to come forward and pose as stern, independent arbiters of our destiny who resist any passing movement in the minds of the electorate?

The gravamen of the charge. Indeed the gravamen of the charge that I make against the House of Lords is that they are developing a studied habit of caucus electioneering. I say that so far from standing against gusts of popular passion, they are always endeavouring to play the party game of the Tory Party. When you come to a question like the Licensing Bill, which I am quite ready to admit was not what is called good electioneering, but which was an earnest effort to grapple with one of the most awful social evils, when you come to a measure like that, when the House of Lords think they can score an unworthy popularity with certain sections by rejecting it, then whatever appeals are made to them by the best men in the House of Lords, whatever compromises are offered by the Government, whatever appeals are addressed to them by the Churches, they brush it out of existence in one moment because they are hoping to get, not a gust of public passion, but a gust of public-house passion.

The claim for aristocracies. 'All civilization,' said Lord Curzon, quoting Renan, 'all civilization has been the work of aristocracies.' They liked that in Oldham. There was not a duke, not an earl, not a marquis, not a viscount in Oldham who did not feel that a compliment had been paid to him. What does Lord Curzon mean by aristocracy? It is quite clear from the argument of his speech that he did not mean nature's aristocracy, the best and most gifted beings in each generation in each country, the wisest, the bravest, the most generous, the most skilful, the most beautiful, the strongest, and the most virtuous. If he had meant that I think we should probably agree with him. Democracy has been called 'the association of us all through the leadership of the best'. But the context of Lord Curzon's quotation and the argument of his speech, which was designed entirely to prove that the House of Lords was a very desirable institution for us to maintain in its present form, clearly shows that by aristocracy he meant the hereditary legislators, the barons, earls, dukes, etc., and their equivalents in other countries. That is what he meant by aristocracy in the argument he employed at Oldham. Again I say this has only to be stated to be dismissed as absurd. 'All civilization has been the work of aristocracies.' It would be much more true to say 'The upkeep of aristocracies has been the hard work of all civilizations.'

'We trust the people.' The House of Lords have struck their blow. What is our answer going to be? Our answer is to advise the sovereign to dissolve Parliament. It is we who have appealed to the electorate. There were other courses which a Government possessed of a great majority in the House of Commons could have taken. There were very strong arguments in favour of some of these courses, and there were many high constitutional authorities who thought that we could have used the great power which a House of Commons majority undoubtedly possesses against the House of Lords at this juncture. We take the simplest course. We do not wish to have power unless the nation wishes us to have it, and we do not intend to undertake the burden and responsibility of Government unless full and effective powers are given to us. We trust the people, and we come to you.

THE PEOPLE'S BUDGET

The Budget in the Commons. For six months the Budget has been before the country. For seventy Parliamentary days and nights it has been debated in the House of Commons. There have been 554 divisions upon specific points of principle and difference. I don't suppose there ever was a Bill which was more shaped and moulded by Parliamentary debate, or which has received a greater measure of Parliamentary time and attention. Months of patient care have been consumed in trying to meet objections, in trying to win the largest possible measure of agreement for this great scheme. Scores of concessions, some of the first importance, have been introduced to meet the wishes of particular classes of opponents. Upon the work of examining the Budget hundreds of members of Parliament, each of whom is responsible for a constituency upon the average of about 10,500 electors, have been engaged all this time, and have sacrificed cheerfully their leisure, their health, and in two cases, it might almost be said, have sacrificed their lives. The work of the Ministers engaged upon the Budget has been severe almost beyond parallel, and they have been aided by the continuous efforts of an enormous staff of Civil Servants, actuaries, lawyers, accountants, and officials. Through all this prodigious labour we have ploughed our way, upon the whole with undisturbed good temper on both sides, and without the employment of any guillotine procedure for shortening debate.

The Lords and the Bill. Now we are at the end of that long job. The Budget Bill has left the House of Commons; it has left it in its final form. It has left the House of Commons, backed by the unbroken majority of the whole of the Liberal, Radical, and Labour forces. The most moderate men and the most advanced, the most daring and the most cautious, are united at the end of this great measure in reasoned and well-weighed agreement. Such a spectacle of cohesion and party unity at the end of a great task like this is in itself almost unexampled in the history of British politics. All that has been done, and now we are told that it is to count for nothing, that the fruits of all this toil and perseverance, of all this knowledge and authority, of all this immense and well-informed discussion, are, after a few perfunctory hours of speech-making, to be swept incontinently out of existence by a House of hereditary lords, a small proportion of whom no doubt have some general acquaintance with the provisions of the Budget, but the vast majority of whom do not understand either the proposals or the arguments by which those proposals are advocated or opposed, and the great majority of whom have certainly not taken the trouble to read the Bill they are about to destroy. I ask you first of all this evening to consider that fact with the attention it deserves. When you consider on the one hand the prolonged discussions in the House of Commons, and on the other hand the swift, contemptuous rejection which we are told awaits the Budget Bill in the House of Lords, I say without hesitation that the elected representatives of any democracy have never been treated with more presumptuous contumely. Why, the French nobility before the Revolution never regarded the feeble Parliament of Paris with more disdain than the British Peers are going to show to the oldest, the most famous, and, as they have yet to learn, the most powerful representative assembly in the world.

No 'tacking'. Such action cannot for one moment be justified on the ground that the Budget contains irrelevant and
unnecessary matter tacked on to it. It cannot be alleged that
the House of Commons have, in the words of the House of
Lords' resolution of 1702, 'annexed any clause or clauses to
a Bill of aid and supply, the matter of which is foreign to or
different from the matter of a money Bill'. That is not true.
Not a line in the Finance Bill can be pointed to which is not
absolutely necessary for the proper levying of the taxes
authorized by it. If there ever is to be a tax on the unearned
increment in land, the machinery we propose, or similar
machinery, would be absolutely essential, and must be proposed as an integral part of the tax. As for liquor licences,
they have always been dealt with in the Budget. No one has
ever dreamed of suggesting that they are, to quote the Lords,
a subject 'foreign to the matter of a money Bill'. Of all the
allegations that of 'tacking' is the most trumpery and the
most insincere. But then, it is said, 'Look at the speeches
of the Chancellor of the Exchequer and the President of the
Board of Trade.' Well, I am very glad the House of Lords
should look at those speeches. They may hear what is called
'something to their advantage'. But fancy making a revolution on account of a speech! That such a pretence should be
put forward, if that is to be the reason for the action of the
House of Lords, only shows how utterly unfit those persons
are to have any concern with serious affairs.

No emergency. Nor can the rejection of the Budget be
justified, or even excused, by alleging any circumstances of
emergency at the present time. There are no circumstances
of emergency. Of course, rich people do not like being made
to pay heavier taxes any more than poor people; of course,
licence-holders do not relish the prospect of having to pay a
larger rent to the State for the valuable monopoly they have

hitherto enjoyed upon such easy terms; of course, the landlords do not like the idea of a valuation of land — it will
reveal the truth for the first time about the land monopoly.
All that is quite natural. It may not be very noble, but it is
quite natural and it is quite human. I can easily understand
why these classes oppose the Budget and wish to overturn
the Government. But if they believe, as they tell us they do
believe, that the taxes are bad and will be found to be unworkable and unpopular in practice, and that the people are
with them, and will be more on their side the more they realize what our policy really means — if they believe that, there
can be no necessity for the adoption of such a violent measure
as the rejection of the Budget at the present moment.

Nothing in the Budget irrevocable. Nothing in the Budget is
irrevocable. There is a Budget every year. Every Government presents its estimates of expenditure, and if the people
don't agree to the taxes the Government can soon be changed.
The Conservative Party would come into power in the ordinary course. If that were so they would become responsible,
having obtained a majority in the regular way in the constituencies, and then they would have a right to put forward
their plan, whatever it was. Nothing in this Budget is irrevocable. Nothing is contained in the Budget which cannot
be altered in another Budget.

The cost of valuation. Of course, it is quite true that if after
two years of work on the valuation scheme a Government
were returned to power which was opposed to all forms of
land taxation — if that is the decision of the British people —
it is quite true that then the money which had been spent up
to date upon the valuation would be wasted. That is a
serious matter; I do not underrate it in the least. I think the
waste of public treasure should justly excite the concern of

every citizen. But how many more millions of public money and of national credit will be wasted by the rejection of the Budget and by the consequent disorganization of the financial system and the disturbance of trade which must follow therefrom? If it be sought to argue, as some of my Conservative friends argue, that the valuation cannot be stopped hereafter, whatever the nation decide, without waste of money, and that consequently valuation once begun would be practically irrevocable — if that is the argument, my answer is that the desperate remedy which the Lords propose to apply to prevent this possible and problematical waste of money in the future, will necessarily and instantly involve a far greater destruction of public wealth than that which, we are informed, the House of Lords are anxious to avoid.

Impatience for the so-called sweets of office. Nothing in the Budget is irrevocable. They had only to wait until, in the regular course, the present Parliament came to an end, and then, if the electors agreed with them — as the Tories say they believe — a Conservative Government could put all the old things back in all the old places. And how long would they have had to wait? Why, you can scarcely credit it. This Parliament has already lived more than two-thirds of its statutory life. Six sessions, which is their *maximum*, would have been completed in less than two years from now. Very likely six sessions would not have been completed. The early months of 1911 might have seen and would probably have seen a general election. If, as they declare, the nation is on the side of the Conservative Party, if the majority of the public are longing to return them to power, thirsting to see them back again, they would only have had to wait fifteen months, or at the outside twenty-two months, before tasting the so-called sweets of office and fingering those official seals for which their palms are itching. It is because they cannot bear to wait fifteen months that the British Constitution is to be torn and rent.

The only persons fit to serve the Crown. This proud Tory faction think they are the only persons fit to serve the Crown. They regard government as their perquisite and political authority as a mere adjunct to their wealth and titles. They cannot bear to see a Government in power representative of and resting on the middle and working classes, a Government supported by the nonconformists and the trade unions, which cares nothing, and less than nothing for the fashionable influences before which they have always bowed. And just as they clung to office under Mr Balfour to the last possible minute, long after honour and power had departed from them, so now they grab and clutch at the tempting morsel in all the indecent precipitation of ungovernable appetite. They could not bear to wait till the dish came round to them in the regular order. They must needs kick over the table in their gluttonous haste.

We shall not cling to office; we have no reason to fear the people. What shall we do? I will tell you what we shall not do. We shall not cling to office. We have no reason to fear the English people. We shall not be content to bear the burden and to face the responsibility of conducting the government unless we have full and effective power. There are few spectacles more contemptible in public life, and none, I think, more pitiful, than that of a Ministry, or a Minister, willing to accept and bear great responsibility without adequate power to sustain that responsibility. No, we shall not cling to office, but, backed by you, we shall strike with all our strength. If the nation does not sustain us effectively, then by all means let others take up the burden — let them find the money; and if we are returned in the future victorious, then I say to you in all seriousness tonight that we shall be bound to take the necessary steps to make sure that what the House of Lords are going to do in the next few days will never be done again.

The practical consequences of rejection. If the condemnation of the Peers rejecting the Budget depended upon the customs and maxims of the past and upon the recorded opinions of famous statesmen, the case against them would already be overwhelming. No fair-minded jury, no competent Court, would say they had any constitutional right or any moral excuse. But there is a much more homely way of proving that rejection is an act of violence against the Constitution. The practical consequences which would follow the rejection are the best and simplest proof that it is an act unnatural and unprecedented in all workings of the Constitution. What will the consequences be? The financial apparatus by which the money to pay the nation's bill is raised will be thrown out of gear and broken into confusion. The liabilities have been and are being incurred; the money is being spent; the soldiers and the sailors are earning their pay; the ships of war — those vessels which we were told a few months ago by these same Tories were vital to the safety of the country — are being built; the school teachers, the postmen, the Custom and Excise officers, the Civil Servants, the Old-Age Pensioners — all these have to be maintained from day to day. The whole vast mechanism of a modern State is in full and active operation. The bill to pay all this is now due. It has got to be paid, and it has got to be paid speedily. It is the House of Commons and the House of Commons alone which is called upon to provide the means of payment, just as it is the House of Commons and the House of Commons alone which determines the scale of the expenditure.

The constitutional duty of the Peers. The constitutional form is crudely simple. It is a doctrine older than the Stuarts, older than the Tudors. It goes right back to the hoary times of Henry IV. The Crown demands a grant of supply. The Commons makes the grant, and the Lords assent to the grant. The Commons are bound to make the grant. If they do not make the grant for the expenditure they have authorized other Commons must be got who will; and never since the Civil War have the Commons, even in the most turbulent periods of our party history, even in the days of the coalition between Lord North and Mr Fox — never have they dared to refuse supply to the Crown. The Commons are bound to grant supply, and the Lords are bound to consent to the grant. It is their constitutional duty to assent. They have no right of dissent. How can they dissent? They do not fix the expenditure; no estimates are laid before them; no estimates are examined by them; no financial statement is submitted to them by the executive. They cannot forbid or authorize the spending of a single penny. They have no power to regulate the expenditure; they have no power to determine how that expenditure can be met. If they destroy the Budget they cannot propose another in its place. They cannot provide a single tax to meet the gap of one they sweep out of existence. Liabilities have been incurred; the House of Lords has even assented to the liabilities by passing the Appropriation Bill for the year. The money must be found. All the House of Lords can do — if they go mad — is to put a stone on the track and throw the train of State off the line, and that is what they are going to do.

The power of the Peers in finance is only a power to wreck. And after it is all over, after the agitation has spoiled the Christmas trade, after we have had the decision of the nation, whatever it may be, after all the tumult and the shouting, the money will still have to be found. After, in their fury, they have sworn at the hotel-keeper and cuffed the waiter and smashed up the coffee-room, the Bill will be there just the same. No, it will be larger, because of the damage, and that Bill some Government, or some party, in some way or other, has got to meet before March 31st. The best proof that the House of Lords have no right, moral or constitutional, to touch finance or reject the Budget lies in the direct consequence of their action. They claim the right to steer the ship. All they can do is to run her on the rocks. Mischief indefinite and illimitable is within their power, but to limit the evil or repair the damage is utterly beyond their power. For that they have to turn to the House of Commons. Their right to intervene in finance is only a right to wreck finance, and that is no right at all in any Court that ever sat; and if every other body of men in the British Empire were to use their powers to wreck and to smash in the same furious and sordid spirit as we are told these rich and fortunate men are going to do, then very soon there would be very little British Constitution and very little British Empire for any one to enjoy.

Finance is the key to power. It is finance and finance alone which has given the House of Commons — that is to say, the only assembly over which you have any control whatever — its power in the State. By judicious and valiant use of this money power the House of Commons converted the old despotism of the Stuarts into the safe, enduring, constitutional monarchy which we all honour today. By a further use of that power the eighteenth-century oligarchy was gradually transformed into the broad democratic State which we all enjoy — for the present. It is that power, which belongs to the people's House alone, which makes our Constitution democratic in a real and genuine sense, and which gives everyone a share — a small share, no doubt, but still a precious share — in the affairs of his country. The House of Commons, freely chosen to represent the electors, is the power which shapes policy and makes and maintains administrations.

The House of Lords is representative of nobody. The House of Lords, on the other hand, is representative of nobody. Most of its members are there because of the accident of birth. A few have more recent and some have more questionable titles. They are representative of nobody; they are inaccessible to argument. The vast majority never attend to their duties at all. I have had a calculation made. It was a very long and tiresome calculation. I have had all the divisions for the last fifty years in the House of Lords examined, and I find that out of more than 600 Peers only 103 on the average voted in the divisions of the last fifty years. Nearly all of the Peers belong to the Carlton Club; nine out of ten of them are Conservatives. Nearly all of them represent the interests of property, and nearly all, mind you, one particular kind of property — property in land. I cannot believe that in the twentieth century the British people are by their deliberate vote going to constitute this assembly — a fraction of whom no doubt are men of real eminence and dignity, but the great majority of whom are quite ordinary people of the well-to-do class with all the narrowest prejudices and special interests of that class — I cannot believe that you by your votes are going to constitute them the main foundation on which the governing power in our land is reposed. I cannot believe the middle classes and the working classes, who after all have only to use their voting strength to get their own way, are going to degrade and cast away their own voting powers which their fathers won for them in the past,

C

which they value so highly at present, and which they are
bound in honour to hand on uninjured to their children's
children — I cannot believe that the electors are going obse-
quiously to hand over their most vital constitutional right,
namely, to choose the Chamber that governs the Government, to an antiquated body of titled persons utterly beyond
their control.

The aim of the Lords. But that would be the consequence of
the House of Lords securing at a general election the absolute
constitutional right not only to destroy any legislation they
dislike, but also to throw out a Budget. For what would be
the position? Whatever Government we have must be
responsible; it must have power to raise the money to meet
the obligations of the year. The very day the Budget is
introduced the immense process of collecting the taxes begins, and all the policies and all the plans of every department in the State are based upon it. So nicely are things
calculated that an extra Sunday even, or a spell of hot
weather, or a wet season, makes a difference in the yield,
which makes its effect in the calculation and in the consequences at the other end. One of the most indispensable
things to good government is the sure and regular collection
of the taxes. But if the House of Lords establish their right
to reject the Budget of the year whenever it may happen to
receive it, then the whole of this tremendous process by
which the king's revenue is raised will lie in complete uncertainty until the autumn of every year. We shall never know
that the House of Lords, before it goes away to the grouse
moors for its autumn holiday, may not take a dislike to the
taxes, or to the Government, or to some other part of the
policy of Government — their foreign policy, their naval
policy, or social policy as it may be — and then themselves,
themselves being the sole judges in the case, declare that

the Budget is a revolution, whatever a revolution is, or that the Chancellor of the Exchequer is a Socialist, whatever a Socialist is, or that there has been tacking, whatever tacking is, and that in consequence there must be a general election before the money can be raised.

The consequences of the Peers' action. Now that is not the way in which any country can be managed. It is not a plan upon which any administration can be carried on. No body of honourable men would be responsible for carrying on the king's Government on terms like that unless they not only had a majority, as hitherto, in the House of Commons, but could depend upon a majority to pass the Budget in the House of Lords as well; and consequently and inevitably the House of Lords would become the main source of power in the State and the centre from which, under the Crown, Governments were made and unmade. And when you hear it said that all the House of Lords wish to do is to ascertain the true will of the people, do not be deceived. You will find, I expect, that there is nothing they will like less than the true will of the people. They do not wish to ascertain the true will of the people. They want to escape the Budget and to destroy the Government. Such is their aim, and to do this they have resolved to violate the Constitution in a manner which, if they succeed, will infallibly leave them the predominant authority in the State. By interfering with finance they usurp the rights of the House of Commons; by claiming to force a dissolution they usurp the prerogative of the Crown, for it is the Crown alone that can determine a dissolution; and by refusing supplies, they strike at the whole structure of civil government and of national safety.

No compromise. Such are the issues with which we are face to face. But we may, I think, take up our stations before the conflict, not only in that good conscience which enables men to be serene amid the hazards of war, but with well-grounded hopes of securing the victory. The reports which we receive from town and country, the strength of our united and unbroken party, the plain, resolute guidance of our leader, the Prime Minister, all justify a confident expectation of success. Our adversaries in their frenzy have offered us battle on the worst possible ground for them, and at the worst possible moment. We will meet them without delay. Now is the appointed time. Never since the triumphant passage of the great Reform Bill have the House of Lords and the British people met face to face at a general election. More than once in the seventy-five years which have passed since then the struggle has come very near; but always something, some compromise, some hesitation, some delay, has intervened to avert it. Nothing will avert it now. There will be no hesitation, there will be no delay, there will be no compromise. The nation must choose for itself. We await their decision with confidence. We do not base our hopes on party calculations, encouraging though these may be; we base them on our faith in the wisdom and genius of the British people, and on the power which that people have always shown to rise to the height of great emergencies, and to defend against invasion and insult the primary rights and freedoms of their race.

The actual proposals of the Budget. You are, no doubt, generally acquainted with them. There is the increase in the income-tax of twopence, the further discrimination between earned and unearned income, and the super-tax of sixpence on incomes of over £5,000 a year. There are the increases in estate duties and in the legacy duties, and there are the new duties on stamps; there is the tax on motor cars and petrol, the proceeds of which are to go to the improvement of the

roads and the abatement of the dust nuisance; there are the
taxes on working class indulgences — namely, the increase
in the tax on tobacco and on whisky, which enable the working man to pay his share, as indeed he has shown himself
very ready to do; there are the taxes on liquor licences,
which are designed to secure for the State a certain special
proportion of the monopoly value created wholly by the
State and with which it should never have parted; and,
lastly, there are the three taxes upon the unearned increment
in land, upon undeveloped land, upon the unearned increment in the reversion of leases, and then there is the tax upon
mining royalties.

Now these are the actual proposals of the Budget, and I
do not think that, if I had the time, I should find any great
difficulty in showing you that there are many good arguments, a great volume of sound reason, which can be adduced
in support of every one of these proposals. Certainly there
is no difficulty in showing that since the Budget has been
introduced there has been no shock to credit, there has been
no dislocation of business, there has been no set-back in the
beginning of that trade revival about the approach of which
I spoke at the beginning of the year, and which is now actually in progress. The taxes which have been proposed have
not laid any burden upon the necessaries of life like bread or
meat, nor have they laid any increased burden upon comforts like tea and sugar. There is nothing in these taxes which
makes it harder for a labouring man to keep up his strength
or for the small man of the middle class to maintain his style
of living. There is nothing in these taxes which makes it
more difficult for any hard-working person, whether he
works with his hands or his head, to keep a home together in
decent comfort. No impediment has been placed by these
taxes upon enterprise; no hampering restrictions interrupt
the flow of commerce. On the contrary, if the tax upon spirits

should result in a diminution in the consumption of strong drink, depend upon it, the State will gain, and all classes will gain. The health of millions of people, the happiness of hundreds of thousands of homes, will be sensibly improved, and money that would have been spent upon whisky will flow into other channels, much less likely to produce evil and much more likely to produce employment. And if the tax on undeveloped land, on land, that is to say, which is kept out of the market, which is held up idly in order that its owner may reap unearned profit by the exertions and through the needs of the surrounding community, if that tax should have the effect of breaking this monopoly and of making land cheaper, a tremendous check on every form of productive activity will have been removed. All sorts of enterprises will become economically possible which are now impossible owing to the artificially high price of land, and new forces will be liberated to stimulate the wealth of the nation.

The money must be found. I say we have put forward our plan. By the immense labours of a six months' session, after six or seven hundred hours of discussion, and after 550 divisions on specific points of principle, our Budget has been placed before the country and before the House of Lords. That Budget provided for the present need, and it did more. It would have provided — and it will yet provide — for the growing needs of the future. It would have provided not merely for the public charges as we see them at present, but in future years the expanding yield of the same taxes, without addition or further disturbance, would have enabled us to finance an expansive and a fruitful social programme. For the moment all has been swept away. Supplies have been refused. Finances have been paralysed. A Parliament has been destroyed. And we are come to you. Another Budget, after the election is over, must come on the heels of this one. Not merely will the sixteen millions have to be found, but provision must be made for the increasing cost of next year's administration. So that, although our Budget for the moment has been destroyed by the House of Lords, the need — the plain, unquestioned need — which called that Budget forth remains and must be met.

Will the foreigner pay? Of course, the first thing that will be said, I have no doubt, will be that they will find the money by taxing the foreigner. I hope you will not expect me to waste much time with that mischievous and foolish delusion. I think it is a safe general rule to say that every tax which a British Chancellor of the Exchequer can impose will be paid by the people of Great Britain and Ireland; for I think that, broadly speaking, it is true that any tax — except a tribute exacted by force from a conquered nation — that any tax invented by any Government in any country in any age will ultimately be paid by the people of that country.

Only two ways of obtaining wealth — production or plunder. After all, I am not sorry that we cannot tax the foreigner.

There are only two ways of obtaining wealth in this world, by production and by plunder. Part of the funds of each nation are legitimately taken by the State for its maintenance; but that the finances of this powerful country should stand on so paltry and pitiful a basis as that of the filching of a million or two from the labour of neighbouring nations with whom we traffic would be utterly contemptible if it were not utterly absurd. I do not deny that a State can for a moment, in exceptional cases and in regard sometimes to peculiar commodities, add to its revenue by sudden and unexpected changes in fiscal policy. Like the Arabs of the desert, who pounce down from their mountains upon some unsuspecting caravan and make good their retreat with their booty, these fortuitous and temporary gains can sometimes be secured. But what is the result? Other caravans choose other roads, or travel under better escort, and the Arabs remain the poor inhabitants of the desert.

The revenues upon which we live must come from British pockets. Between Great Britain and Germany, let us say, you have the buyers and the sellers at work. Each side has its natural advantages. Each side seeks to arrive at the true competitive price by the correct higgling of the market. Into this elaborate process comes the British Government with a demand for a million or two of money for purposes quite unconnected with prices and unrelated to trade.

And we are invited to believe that it is not till such interference of Government has taken place that the true price can be reached between buyers and sellers. That is a proposition I have never been able to accept. A temporary gain may follow in certain peculiar circumstances, but it will be utterly insignificant in amount, and only but of brief duration. And as soon as the market turns in favour of the foreigner, the fleeting gain will be wrested back and the tax, whether import or export, together with the whole cost of collection, will be paid in the end by our own people; if they be buyers, they pay in quantity, in quality, or in price; if they be sellers they suffer in profit, convenience, or reserve power. The revenues upon which we live must come from British pockets, and all other language is mere folly and deception.

You can tax wealth or tax wages. Now, if I carry you with me, the revenue on which we live must come from British pockets, then what class and what commodities shall we select to raise the sixteen millions and more which the State immediately requires?

Your choice is severely limited. You have only two courses open to you. You can tax wealth or you can tax weekly wages. That is the whole choice of a British Chancellor of the Exchequer. Now, let us look at these alternatives. The capital wealth of Britain is increasing rapidly. Sir Robert Giffen estimated some years ago that the accretion of the capital in this country was between two and three hundred millions a year. I observe that the paid-up capital of registered companies alone has risen from £1,013,000,000 in 1893 to £2,123,000,000 in 1908. The valuation of estates subject to death duties has increased by eight per cent. The number of estates which come within the range of death duties has increased by eighteen per cent, and that in spite of some avoidance. The most remarkable of all the figures are the figures of the growth of the income tax. The income-tax assessments which come within the range of the Treasury Commissioners have risen from £762,000,000 in 1898-9 to £980,000,000 a year in 1908-9. That is to say, they have risen by £218,000,000. Now, I will make a great deduction from that for a more efficient collection, due largely to the spread of joint-stock enterprise. I am willing to make a deduction, not of one-third, which would probably be accurate, but of one-half. Then, let us say the amount of income assessable for income tax has increased by £109,000,000 in the last ten years.

The ever-increasing luxury of our country—the rapid accumulation of capital. And I think we see the proof of that increase in the ever-increasing luxury of our country, in the ever-increasing numbers — glad I am that it should be so — of wealthy and well-to-do people, who are the amazement of the foreign visitor and the envy of foreign countries. Now, we do not think it excessive to ask of these rapidly growing funds of accumulated wealth at this juncture in our national history a further contribution of about £7,500,000 to £8,000,000 a year — about equal to the cost of four of these Dreadnoughts these same classes were clamouring so loudly for — less than a one-fifteenth part of the increased income of the last ten years; and less, and much less, than the increased annual income of the income-tax-paying classes in a single year. But the House of Lords, which is entirely composed of the classes who are affected by the taxation of wealth, refused to accept the burden.

The comparatively slow advance of wages. Look elsewhere. The wages of ten millions who make returns to the Board of Trade — including the aristocracy of labour — the wages of these ten millions have risen by about £10,000,000 in the last ten years. They are getting £10,000,000 this year more than they got ten years ago. The income-tax assessments have advanced £109,000,000 in the ten years, and the wages of these ten million people have only advanced £10,000,000. Now, £10,000,000 divided among 10,000,000 is £1 a head. But £109,000,000 a year divided among 1,100,000 income-tax payers is more than £100 a head. You have, therefore, to choose between taking the millions which are needed for the defence of the realm and for the social advance of the people from this great fund of capital, which has increased among its possessors to the extent of, on the average, £100 a year per head, on the one hand, or by going to the £1 per head, which in the same period is all that has been secured by the wage-earners.

Capital and wages and the Free Trade system. Let me turn aside to examine for one moment a reflection which will probably arise in your minds, and which will excite comment outside. It is an irrelevant reflection, but it is one which if not dealt with at this point in my argument, may be used to darken counsel. It will be said, do you think that these two processes that you have described — the rapid accumulation of capital and the comparatively slow advance of wages — do you think that they are a satisfactory tribute to the workings of your Free Trade system? My answer to that shall be a succession of facts.

Wages are, on the whole, substantially better in this country than in the protected countries of Europe. First, wages on the whole are substantially better in this country than they are in the protected countries of Europe.

The prices of food are better. The prices of food in this country are much better than they are in the protected countries of Europe. So that the purchasing power of wages in this country is greater than in Europe.

The general condition of wage-earners is better. The general condition of the wage-earners, although there is a very miserable minority in our country — a minority, perhaps, who suffer more than any other equal body in the world — the general condition of the great masses of the wage-earners in this country is superior to the condition of their fellows in Germany, in Italy, or in France.

The rich favour Protection. Fourth, the rich in every country favour Protection; and in every country they say they favour Protection to benefit the poor.

The poor are opposed to Protection. And, fifthly, the poor in every country, in Germany and in the United States especially, are opposed to Protection because they know it cheats and taxes them, and bleeds them at a hundred points.

The man who believes that the wealthy landowners and manufacturers are shouting for Tariff Reform in the interest of the toiler carries simple faith too far. The disproportion between the rewards of capital and labour, which is now evident in every modern country, and which, I think, is not decreasing, and the uneven distribution of wealth, may be grave evils, but they will not be removed by the abandonment of our Free Trade system, and they will only be aggravated by the adoption of a Protectionist system. I always admire trustfulness and simple faith whenever I see them, but I must say that the man who believes that all these wealthy landowners and manufacturers who have banded themselves together with the Tariff Reform League, and who are shouting for Tariff Reform, are doing it in the interests of the toiler and in order to redress the existing inequalities between wealth and poverty — I must say the man who believes that is carrying trustfulness and simple faith a little too far.

The alternative Budget. Let me return to the alternative Budget. Those who put forward the alternative Budget conceal themselves as far as possible in clouds of vapours. They don't want to be too clear and precise, and they want to let it be thought that everyone will gain something and no one will have to pay any contribution. They are in favour of a tax on leather in Bermondsey, but they don't say so much about it in Leicester. They are in favour of taxing foreign goods in English manufacturing centres, but they are a little chary of pressing their case about import duties in a great seaport town. But, after all, certain facts have emerged very plainly from the brilliant clouds of mystery in which they have enshrouded their operations. It is clear that they mean to put Protective import duties on food and on foreign manufactures. Mr Chamberlain, when he undertook his campaign, was very clear about that. Mr Chaplin has on several occasions persuaded the National Union of Conservative Associations to declare in favour of it. Mr Balfour has toed the line. Lord Milner and Lord Lansdowne openly avow their intention of creating a Protective tariff. I am here to tell you that although their intentions may be unmistakable, they will not obtain the money to meet the revenue deficiency with which we are face to face by any taxes they have yet proposed or mentioned.

Taxes on corn and meat depart from the principle of equality of sacrifice. Mr Chamberlain said in the House of Commons, that the taxes on corn and meat would be paid to the extent of three-quarters by the working classes. There are special objections to such taxes. They are not fair taxes, because they depart from the principle of equality of sacrifice, which is the root principle of all fair and just taxation, because bread and meat form a so much larger proportion of the expenditure of the wage-earning man than they do of his richer fellow-countryman. This is especially true of corn, because corn is one of the very few things the consumption of which is increased, not diminished, by a tax. The consumption of corn is increased by a tax because people must have bread, unless they are driven to altogether lower kinds of food; and if bread costs more it is not the bread they do without — what they do without is the piece of meat, or some other more expensive article of food, and even buy more bread to make up for it.

A tax on corn especially unfair on the poor. That is why a tax on corn is especially unfair to the poor and the poorest of the poor, because it not only takes a larger proportion of their earnings from them, but as it operates it tends to aggravate the disproportion in which they are forced to pay it.

Tory pledges as to taxation of food. Let me read you some of the pledges which Mr Chamberlain, Mr Balfour, Mr Bonar Law, and the Tariff Reformers, and the Tory newspapers generally, have given, that whatever money they raise by taxing corn and meat shall be given back in reductions on tea, sugar, and tobacco. Mr Chamberlain, at the Constitutional Club, on June 26th, 1903, said that if the increased cost of bread is met by a proportionate decrease on some other articles of consumption or necessaries for the comfort of life, then in that case, although the price of some articles may be raised, the cost of living will not be increased in the slightest degree. And, again, 'If, for instance, the working classes are called upon to pay 3d. a week additional on the cost of their bread, they may be fully relieved by a reduction of a similar amount in the cost of their tea, their sugar, or even of their tobacco. In this case, what is taken out of one pocket will be put back into the other.' Again, Mr Chamberlain, at Glasgow, October 6th, 1903, 'I propose to take off three-fourths of the duty on tea and half of the duty on sugar, with a corresponding reduction on cocoa and coffee.'

Reiterated pledges. And then at Newcastle — I quote this, not for the purpose of attacking Mr Chamberlain at all, but because they are the solemn pledges of the Tariff Reform Party at Newcastle, October 20th, 1903, 'I am not asking you to raise the amount of taxation in this country, but I am asking you to transfer the taxation from one article to another — from one pocket to another'. And again. 'All these millions which come from the pockets of the foreigner —' only a little while ago they were coming from the pockets of the wage-earner — 'we will give you back — back' — I thought they came from the foreigner — 'in reductions upon your tea and on your sugar, and I hope upon your tobacco.' Now, I quote Mr Bonar Law, at Aberdeen, October 24th,

1905, 'Let us assume', he said, 'that the whole of the import duty be added to the price of the loaf, even then the evil is surely a small one. Revenue must be raised in some way, and if a certain amount of taxation is raised on corn a similar amount of taxation could be taken off something else.'

As for the official leaflets of the Tariff Reform League, their name is legion, and their declarations are precise beyond doubt. Leaflet 104: 'Instead of putting the duties on tea, and upon coffee and sugar and tobacco, we could put them on foreign corn, meat and butter.' Leaflet 116: 'The proposals of the Tariff Reformers are as follows: — (1) To put certain small duties on foreign goods which compete with goods of British production; (2) to tax to a sufficient amount tea, coffee, sugar, and cocoa, to counterbalance new duties on competitive imports of foreign agricultural produce.'

Why is it necessary to counterbalance these duties if the foreigner is going to pay them? Why it should be necessary to counterbalance these duties, if the foreigner is going to pay them our Tariff Reform logician alone understands. Leaflet 117 of the Tariff Reform League: 'Tariff Reform will take off a large part of the heavy taxes on tea, sugar, tobacco, and other articles of food and necessaries of life not grown in this country.'

Mr Balfour's pledges. Now, to come to Mr Balfour: Mr Balfour's conversion to Tariff Reform is always supposed to date from the Birmingham conference of November 14th, 1907. There he laid down what he called 'four practically incontrovertible principles' which were to guide the proposed broadening of the basis of taxation. The first, he said, was that duties should be widespread; the second is that they should be small; the third, that they should not touch raw material; the fourth—note this incontrovertible principle—is 'that they should not alter the proportion'—the *proportion*, mind you—'in which the working classes were asked to contribute to the cost of government.' And then, again, as recently as November 17th, 1909, at the Free Trade Hall, Manchester, Mr Balfour said, 'Certainly I should never have touched Tariff Reform, never given my adhesion to any fiscal change of importance, which was either calculated to, or could, increase the cost—the ordinary cost—the ordinary Budget expenditure of the working classes in this country.' I think you will admit that this is a pretty formidable list of pledges.

Do these pledges stand? What I want to ask is this—I think it is a question that should be asked—do these pledges stand or do they not? Are the Conservative Party to give back in reductions of tea, sugar, and tobacco whatever money they raise by the taxation of bread and meat? Do they adhere to their intention to make those counterbalancing reductions, or were all their pledges of what is called 'frigid and calculated' description?

If the Tories do not intend to break their pledges they have made no headway towards meeting the deficit. If they don't intend to break their explicit public pledges, they have made no headway whatever to meet the sixteen millions of deficit in the revenue; and if they do intend to break their pledges the sooner that is made public the better. They have to choose between bankruptcy and fraud.

What a ten per cent duty really means. Remember we are trying to meet a deficit of £16,000,000. A ten per cent duty on foreign manufactures would yield at first sight

£14,300,000; that is to say, ten per cent on the whole group
of foreign manufactured and partly manufactured articles
which come into this country. But from this total you would
have to deduct first of all £2,300,000 for the £23,000,000 of
re-exports, which only come here because this is the great
free port of the world, and which we handle and make a profit on and send off to all parts of the globe. If a tax were put
on them they would go elsewhere. It would further have to
be reduced by the 'drawbacks' which would be given to all
our exported finished articles, into the manufacture of
which the taxed raw or semi-manufactured materials had entered. Otherwise your tax on the semi-manufactured article
would cripple your export and your competitive power in
the finished and completed products. It would further have
to be reduced by all the foreign goods shut out by the tax.

Articles shut out do not pay the duty. I should like to submit
to you this — and I hope we can agree — that those articles
which are shut out, do not come in, and so they do not pay
the duty, while those articles that pay the duty, come in,
and so they compete with British labour. Let us assume
that one-third of the articles taxed would be shut out. Mr
F. E. Smith put it higher the other day. He assumed that
one-half would be shut out, but it is clear that that is not a
correct estimate. Then there is the further reduction on
account of preference to the colonies; for I don't suppose
the Tariff Reformers are coming forward to put new extra
taxation on the colonies on the goods they send to our
market here; and, lastly, there is the cost of collection.

The cost of collection. The cost of collection would be simply
enormous. The taxes would have to be levied on 289 separate categories of articles, and each one would have to be
sub-divided into a great number of minor classes. Why,

under the system of French tariffs cotton yarn alone is calculated under no fewer than 450 separate heads. We classify it in our simple method of Customs returns under one. I have no doubt whatever, from the information that comes to me from the great department of which I am the head, that a ten per cent duty on manufactured articles would involve taxation on two or three thousand kinds of separate articles. To deal accurately with these and to allow the proper rebates on colonial imports, and the proper drawbacks on British exports, would involve immense work, and it is calculated that the cost of collection would certainly, at the very least, double the existing charges of the Customs service of this country.

The net yield only five or six million. And when you have made all these great deductions from the £14,300,000 which at first sight appear to be yielded by a ten per cent duty, you will not succeed in obtaining—I say this, having very carefully considered the matter—more than £5,500,000 or £6,000,000 at the outside, or more than £4,500,000 if Mr Smith's assumption that half of the foreign goods would be shut out be adopted. I should like to point out that in order to obtain this you would have to set up a tariff which is as vexatious as any that exists around any foreign country. You would have all the trouble, worry, friction, and inconvenience which is entailed by the great tariffs around Germany and the United States, though you would not be adopting that policy of Protection in its entirety to which these countries adhere.

The stupendous shipping industry of this country a direct result of the tariffs abroad and free ports at home. Consider for a moment the burden which such a duty would put upon the shipping industry. There would have to be exacted a certificate of origin in respect of every parcel landed off every vessel which comes to your shores, to say whether it has come from the colonies or a foreign country, and consequently whether it is entitled to the colonial rebate or not. Now, the marvellous position of the British shipping industry is known to you all. Out of scarcely more than 40,000,000 tons of world's shipping, 17,500,000 tons are possessed by the inhabitants of this small island. Nearly half of the seaborne imports into other countries are carried in British ships, and we build for our own use, and for sale to foreigners, almost as many ships as the whole of the rest of the world put together. That stupendous industry is a direct result of tariffs abroad and free ports at home. I should like you to consider the effects upon the shipbuilding trade of an increase in price of all the small manufactured articles used in shipbuilding; to consider the effects upon the shipping trade of an attempt, an avowed attempt, to reduce the amount and volume of goods carried to and fro across the seas; and to consider the effect upon the dock labourers, and all who are concerned in the business of a great port; and upon the banking, and insurance businesses which are so profitable to us.

Fifty millions from the pockets of the consumer, five millions to the Exchequer. But to put these indirect evils of the protective duty upon one side, and to confine myself only to the direct consequences, I would like to point out to you that there are made in this country, so it is calculated, a thousand million pounds worth every year of fully manufactured goods similar to those foreign goods which would be subject to the ten per cent duty. One of the objects of that duty is to raise prices and so stimulate British industry. If we assume that the prices of those thousand million pounds-worth of goods are raised by only half the amount of the duty, say only five per cent over the whole area, then there will be taken from the pockets of the consumers all over the country fifty millions a year, while only five or six millions would go into the coffers of the Chancellor of the Exchequer. I think it is Ruskin who speaks of 'the wreckers' handful of coin gathered from the shore to which they had lured an argosy'. Such, I think, is the aspect of the five or six millions which might be secured by the ten per cent duty at a cost to the consumer of something like ten times the total yield.

Five millions goes a very small way to meet a deficit of sixteen millions. Such is the aspect these ruinously-gotten gains would wear. And when they had been obtained, let me point out to you that five or six millions a year goes a very small way to meet the deficit of sixteen millions, which is what we have to face. And that deficit would remain after all the schemes of rescuing the old-age paupers from the Poor Law, and after all the schemes of Poor-Law reform, of national insurance against unemployment, sickness, and invalidity — after all these schemes upon which we have been working, and which are now ripe for action, have been thrown ruthlessly overboard. In view of these facts, do you not think that the House of Lords, who know nothing of finance, who never have any estimates submitted to them, who have no responsibility or power to alter or vary the taxation, who cannot propose anything in the place of what they destroy, do you not think they have taken a very heavy responsibility in rejecting a Budget and destroying the provision we have made for the urgent needs of the State?

The character of the Budget. On many grounds we may commend this Budget to the country. It makes provision for the present. It makes greater provision for the future. Indirect taxation reaches the minimum. Food taxation reaches the minimum since the South African war. Certainly the working classes have no reason to complain. Nothing in the Budget touches the physical efficiency and energy of labour. Nothing in it touches the economy of the cottage home. Middle-class people with between £300 and £2,000 a year are not affected in any considerable degree, except by the estate duties, and in that not to a large extent, while in some cases they are distinctly benefited in the general way of taxation. The very rich are not singled out for peculiar, special, or invidious forms of imposition.

The chief burden of the increase of taxation is placed upon the main body of the wealthy classes in this country, a class which in number and in wealth is much greater than in any other equal community, if not, indeed, in any other modern State in the whole world. That is a class which, in opportunities of pleasure, in all the amenities of life, and in freedom from penalties, obligations, and dangers, is more fortunate than any other equally numerous class of citizens in any age or in any country. That class has more to gain than any other class of His Majesty's subjects from dwelling amid a healthy and contented people, and in a safely guarded land. I do not agree with the Leader of the Opposition, that they will meet the charges which are placed upon them for the needs of this year by evasion and fraud, and by cutting down the charities which their good feelings have prompted them to dispense. The man who proposes to meet taxation by cutting down his charities, is not the sort of man who is likely to find any very extensive source of economy in the charities which he has hitherto given. As for evasion, I hope those who expect this underrate the public spirit which animates a proportion at any rate of the class which would be most notably affected by the present taxation.

One great assurance. There is for their consolation one great assurance which is worth much more to them than a few millions, more or less, of taxation. It is this — that we are this year taking all that we are likely to need for the policy which is now placed before the country, and which will absorb the energies of this Parliament. And, so far as this Parliament is concerned, it is extremely unlikely, in the absence of a national calamity, that any further demand will be made upon them, or that the shifting and vague shadows of another impending Budget will darken the prospects of improving trade.

Fundamental issues which divide the parties in British politics. When all that may be said on these grounds has been said, we do not attempt to deny that the Budget raises some of the fundamental issues which divide the historic parties in British politics. We do not want to embitter those issues, but neither do we wish to conceal them. We know that the Conservative Party believe that the revenue of the country could be better raised by a Protective tariff. We are confident that a Free Trade system alone would stand the strain of modern needs and yield the expansive power which is necessary at the present time in the revenue. And our proof shall be the swift accomplishment of the fact. Mr Balfour and his friends seek to arrest the tendency to decrease the proportion of indirect to direct taxation which has marked, in unbroken continuity, the course of the last sixty years. We, on the other hand, regard that tendency as of deep-seated social significance, and we are resolved that it shall not be arrested. So far as we are concerned, we are resolved that it shall continue until in the end the entire charge shall be defrayed from the profits of accumulated wealth and by the taxation of those popular indulgences which cannot be said in any way to affect the physical efficiency of labour. The policy of the Conservative Party is to multiply and extend the volume and variety of taxes upon food and necessaries. They will repose themselves, not only, as we are still forced to do, on tea and sugar, but upon bread and meat; not merely upon luxuries and comforts, but also on articles of prime necessity. Our policy is not to increase, but whenever possible to decrease, and ultimately to abolish altogether, taxes on articles of food and the necessaries of life.

One of the climacterics of our national life. If there is divergence between us in regard to the methods by which we are to raise our revenue, there is also divergence in regard to the objects on which we are to spend it. We are, on both sides, inclined to agree that we are approaching, if we have not actually entered on, one of the climacterics of our national life. We see new forces at work in the world, and they are not all friendly forces. We see new conditions abroad and around us, and they are not all favourable conditions; and I think there is a great deal to be said for those who on both sides of politics are urging that we should strive for a more earnest, more strenuous, more consciously national life. But there we part, because the Conservative Party are inclined too much to repose their faith for the future security and pre-eminence of this country upon naval and military preparations, and would sometimes have us believe that you can make this country secure and respected by the mere multiplication of ironclad ships. We shall not exclude that provision, and by our Budget take the steps to secure us that expansion of revenue which will place our financial resources beyond the capacity of any Power that we need to take into consideration.

The strength of great countries is not measured by their material resources. But we take a broader view. We are not going to measure the strength of great countries only by their material resources. We think that the supremacy and predominance of our country depend upon the maintenance of the vigour and health of its population, just as its true glory must always be found in the happiness of its cottage homes. We believe that if Great Britain is to remain great and famous in the world, we cannot allow the present social and industrial disorders, with their profound physical and moral reactions, to continue unchecked. We propose to you a financial scheme, but we also advance a policy of social organization. It will demand sacrifices from all classes; it will give security to all classes. By its means we shall be able definitely to control some of the most wasteful processes in our social life, and without it our country will remain exposed to vital dangers, against which fleets and armies are of no avail.

The Budget necessary. The Budget is necessary. It is absolutely necessary that sixteen millions of money should be raised for the service of the State this year, and a larger sum will be required next year. Does anybody dispute that it is necessary? Will any Conservative come forward and say that the items, the objects for which that taxation is demanded, could be dispensed with? If it were not necessary, do you suppose they would not have been howling from one end of the country to the other? Why, supposing we had incurred this cost through foolish enterprises abroad, or profligate administration at home, the country would have resounded with Conservative complaints at the waste of money of which the Liberal Government had been guilty. But not a dog barks in that direction — not a sound is heard. We scarcely have to defend ourselves at all upon the objects which have given rise to this expenditure. And why? Well do they know the reason why. Some of the cost is due to the Navy. We have made adequate provision, but they are labouring, by working up the most foolish and mischievous panics, to force the Government into an expenditure beyond all that is necessary to maintain the security of the country. And when they are hallooing and exciting themselves and raging furiously together in an endeavour to put the fear of imminent destruction and sudden death into the hearts of the simple-headed folk, who care to listen to them, it is surely not unreasonable that we should ask them to pay their share fairly of the comparatively modest, but still sufficient, armaments which we have thought it necessary to provide.

The Tories and the Navy. The Naval Estimates have risen by three millions this year. I regret it; but I am prepared to justify it. There will be a further increase next year. I regret it; but within proper limits necessary to secure national safety I shall be prepared to justify it; but I hope you will not expect me to advocate a braggart and sensational policy of expenditure upon armaments. I have always been against that, as my father was before me.

His Majesty's Government are resolved that the defensive measures of this country shall be prescribed by the policy of Ministers responsible to Parliament, and by the calculations, subject to that policy, of the experts on whom those Ministers rely, and not by the folly and the clamour of party politicians or sensational journalists. In that determination we as a Government are united, and we shall remain united. Yet it is clear that the increase in the Naval Estimates of this year must be followed by another increase in those of next year. That is deplorable. It will impose upon our finances a strain which some other nations would not find it very easy to bear, but which, if the necessity be proved, this country will not be unwilling, and will certainly not be unable to support.

Well, but what have the Conservative Party got to say about it? Have they any right to complain of the taxes which are necessary for the maintenance of our naval power?

How the need was faced. The need has to be faced, and I think the position occupied by the Chancellor of the Exchequer at the beginning of the year was not one which any man of political experience and of high political position would have been inclined to envy. He was confronted by this heavy deficit, and I think a man of less originality and less pluck would have been baffled and dismayed by the task which lay before him. But not so our friend Lloyd George. He drew out of his difficulties a means of future triumph. Instead of merely making a plan sheepishly to defray the cost of the pensions and of the expenditure that falls due in the present year, he planned to pay not only what we have to pay this year, but it is certain that the taxes which he proposed would bring higher revenues in the following years. And it was from these expanding revenues that we hoped and intended — and if you will allow me to say so — still hope and intend to pay, not merely for the Old-Age Pensions and the Dreadnoughts that have been ordered, but to defray a large constructive interdependent scheme of social organization.

The good financial record of the Government. The financial record of the Government has been a good one. Compared with almost any other Government that has held power in Great Britain, its record is high, and, compared with the financial record of the Government which immediately preceded it, its record is unquestionably superior. In the three years that the finances had been under the control of Mr

Asquith, the present Prime Minister, nearly forty-seven millions of debt had been paid off — war debt accumulated by our predecessors; seven-and-a-half millions of taxes had been remitted, including half the taxation upon sugar, a portion of the taxation upon tea, and all the taxation upon coal. The tax on coal was resented by the whole of the mining community, and undoubtedly damaged our foreign trade in coal. And a remission had also been made — a very important point — upon the lower class of incomes, so that they have some relief in respect of earned income, and a difference is made between earned and unearned income.

Income Tax. There is all the difference in the world between the income which a man makes from month to month or from year to year by his continued exertion, and which may stop at any moment, and will certainly stop if he is incapacitated, and the income which is derived from the profits of accumulated capital, and which is a continuing income irrespective of the exertion of its owner. Nobody wants to penalize or to stigmatize income derived from dividends, rent, or interest; for accumulated capital, apart from monopoly, represents the exercise of thrift and prudence, qualities which are only less valuable to the community than actual service and labour. But the great difference between the two classes of income remains. We are all sensible of it, and we think that that great difference should be recognized when the necessary burdens of the State have to be divided and shared between all classes. The application of this principle of differentiation of income tax has enabled the present Government sensibly to lighten the burden of the great majority of income-tax payers. Under the late Conservative Government about 1,100,000 income-tax payers paid income tax at the statutory rate of a shilling in the pound. Mr Asquith, the Prime Minister, when Chancellor of the Exchequer, reduced the income tax in respect of earned incomes under £2,000 a year from a shilling to ninepence, and it is calculated that 750,000 income-tax payers—that is to say, nearly three-quarters of the whole number of income-tax payers — who formerly paid at the shilling rate, have obtained an actual relief from taxation to the extent of nearly £1,200,000 a year in the aggregate. The present Chancellor of the Exchequer in the present Budget has added to this abatement a further relief — a very sensible relief, I venture to think, you will consider it — on account of each child of parents who possess under £500 a year, and that concession involved a further abatement and relief equal to £600,000 a year. It is founded on the highest principle: authority for it figured in one of the Budget proposals of Mr Pitt, and it is today recognized by the law of Prussia. Taking together the income-tax reforms of Mr Asquith and Mr Lloyd George —taking the two together because they are all part of the same policy, and they are all part of our treatment as a Government of this great subject — taking them together, it is true to say that very nearly three out of every four persons who pay income tax will be taxed after this Budget, this penal Budget, this wicked, monstrous, despoliatory Budget — three out of every four persons will be taxed for income tax at a lower rate than they were by the late Conservative Government.

A fair Budget. I say that the Budget is a fair Budget. It is fair to all classes. I think it is perfectly fair to ask a man who has over £5,000 a year to pay a super-tax of 6d. in the pound on the income which he has over £3,000 per year; and even Mr Balfour says that it is fair, too. We think it quite fair that death duties and legacy duties — which, after all, are based on the oldest principle of taxation which has existed in this country — it is quite fair that property passing at death should pay its due to the State which secures the heir the full enjoyment of it; and it is fair that the due which the State requires should vary within reasonable limits according to the public needs. We think it quite fair that a tax should be put upon motor cars. We think it quite fair to come to the working man and to ask him to bear a tax on spirits and tobacco. I have been told that from a cheap electioneering point of view we should have made a more popular Budget if we had left those out. I don't believe it. I think the working classes would have thought poorly of a Government which was afraid to come to them for their share. It is satisfactory to see that they have paid their share in a manly silence, which is in remarkable contrast to the melancholy cries, the choking sobs, and the pitiful lamentations which arise from the unfortunate millionaires and the mulcted marquises. I claim that the Budget is fairly conceived, and that it met this great public emergency in a straightforward and honest way.

Has the Budget affected the security of property? It is not true that this Budget affects the security of property in our country. Property in Britain is very secure. But it would be a great mistake to suppose that the security of property in this country depended upon the maintenance of the House of Lords. If the security of property depended upon the action of 500 or 600 peers alone, it would have gone long ago. The security depends upon the wide diffusion of property and its increasing spread year by year among new classes and over great numbers of people. That is the first security. The combined interests of millions guarantee the security of property. But property will not be secure for long periods merely because it is gradually diffused more and more widely throughout the nation. There must be another guarantee besides that. It must be supported by the moral convictions of the people, and if the moral convictions of the people are to be retained, then there must be a constant and successful effort to reconcile the processes by which property is acquired with ideas of justice, usefulness, and services to fellow-men. Just laws regulating the acquisition of wealth are the essential foundation, and only permanent foundation, by which the security of property can be based. A society where property was insecure would quickly degenerate into barbarism. A society where property was secure irrespective of the methods by which it was acquired or retained — such a society would be degenerating not merely to barbarism, but to death.

THE PEOPLE'S TRADE

3 THE PEOPLE'S TRADE

The Protective tariffs have warped and restricted the growth of the industries of the nations who have adopted them. I believe myself that Protective tariffs wherever they have been introduced have done harm. I believe they have warped and restricted the growth of the industries of the nations who have adopted them. I believe that they have been unfairly injurious to the poorer classes. I observe that the poorer people both in Germany and in America bitterly resent the high tariffs under which they live. I believe that these tariffs tend to the corruption of public life and of public men; that they make every town and every part of the country send a member to the legislature not to consider the generous and broad interests of the whole country, but to push the particular line of goods and of manufacture in the place from which he comes. I am quite certain that the high food prices which prevail in Germany and the United States are a cruel injury to the hard-working people of those countries.

Protection will not stop unemployment. It is, furthermore, a delusion to suppose that Protective tariffs will stop unemployment. Germany and the United States have high Protective tariffs — far higher than any tariffs yet suggested for us — great tariffs of fifty and sixty per cent, and yet with all their high duties they do not prevent themselves being brought into contact with that grim problem of industrial civilization, the unemployed residuum of the labour market; nor do they prevent those violent fluctuations of the state of trade and of employment which, within the limitations of our present knowledge and our present science of government, baffle the statesmen of every race and every clime.

The working classes to pay three-fourths of the taxes. What have workers to gain from an increase in the cost of food and the ordinary necessaries of life? What have the cardroom operatives in Lancashire, the spinners, and weavers to gain? These are new burdens which will fall directly on them. Mr Chamberlain admitted — I heard him with my own ears — in the House of Commons, in 1903, that the working classes would pay three-fourths of these taxes. Let us be just to Mr Chamberlain. He went on to say that, as they paid that large proportion, it was only fair that it should be given back in Old-Age Pensions. But the Conservative Party came forward there, and made him take Old-Age Pensions out of the Tariff Reform programme. They made him write a letter to the newspapers to say that he had done so. Old-Age Pensions went, and the taxes remained. Then we intervened. We pushed the taxes away and pushed the Pensions forward. You were offered the Pensions contingent upon food taxes; the Pensions have now come without the food taxes, and I should advise the working classes to stick to them without the food taxes.

The taxes will involve a sharp reduction in wages. The proposal which is put forward by the Tariff Reformers is equal to a sharp reduction in the wages of every operative in Lancashire. I challenge anybody to prove that the taxes on meat and bread which are proposed will not involve a reduction in the wages, will not take the form of a shrinkage

D

in the purchasing power, and consequently in the wages,
of every operative in Lancashire. How is the decline in
wages to be adjusted? The margin of profit of the manufacturer is not a large one. There are already keen disputes
as to which way wages should move. I know something of
this from my position at the Board of Trade, and I honestly
hope we may get to some good arrangement of a sliding
scale in that most serious matter for all of you. But such a
change as that proposed, which will fall directly on the wages
of labour, must lead to an increase of trade disputes in the
Lancashire trade, which will be of the very greatest danger
to the permanence of the industry. How the burden is to be
borne, what alteration of wages should be made to make up
to the worker the extra charge in the increased cost of
living, must lead you out into a field of industrial dispute,
which may easily provoke some prolonged strike or great
struggle in the cotton trade; and you know very well that
that can only prove injurious to all your interests, and that
it may entail the loss of old markets, and will certainly bring
about the birth of new competitors. So much for the workers
under this new scheme. What has the Lancashire employer
to gain?

**What has the producer or consumer to gain or lose by a pro-
tective tariff?** Lancashire cotton is supreme. We can beat the
whole world. Our cotton goods overleap tariff walls, even
those of the United States, where the raw cotton is grown.
Our cotton is to the extent of four-fifths an export trade. We
are supreme in neutral markets; we hold with the greatest
ease, without any favour or any preference, the great
markets of India and China. There is practically no foreign
competition at home except in certain special lines. We
enjoy absolute sovereignty in our home markets. What
have the cotton manufacturers to gain by a Protective

tariff? And what have they to lose! Our Protectionist
friends always say to us, 'You ought to think of the producer as well as the consumer.' Well, let us think of the producer. The greatest producer is the greatest consumer. I
wonder if any of those who are connected with the cotton
industry ran their minds over all the articles used in the
day-to-day conduct of a large cotton mill, whether they
could say how much the cost of production would be increased, if every one of the things they used cost only ten
per cent more? If everything — the flour, the leather, the
machinery, the building materials, the paper, the account
books, even the spectacles on the nose of the junior partner
— if all these various articles cost just ten per cent more
what would be the increase to the cost of production? Now
cheapness of production is vital to the cotton trade. It is not
merely if the cost is raised that foreigners will be able to
cut you out. Remember that you serve millions and millions
of poor people in India and China, and if the cost is raised the
demand will fall off immediately; and therefore you of all
other trades in the country would have to pay more for
everything you use and would not be able to recover even a
portion of your loss by charging more for what you sold. Let
our manufacturers in Lancashire consider this. Let them
add to this the reprisals and disturbance which Tariff Reform must entail, and then, I say, even the most conservative amongst you will turn with relief to the Budget of
Mr Lloyd George — that great Budget which the Lords have
rejected but which the people will restore.

The menace. Free Trade is menaced by the Conservative
Party. What is coming in January is not a by-election; not a
by-election where even if the wrong candidate be returned,
at any rate there is a Liberal and Free-Trade Government in
power. No, a mistake at a general election will be irreparable.

A victory of the Tory Party at the general election will mean the immediate erection of a tariff, including the taxation of food, of manufactured articles, and of semi-manufactured articles, which are the raw materials of important industries.

Lancashire's case against Protective tariffs. Let me, then, once again state the unanswered and unanswerable case of Lancashire against any form of Protective tariff. Cotton, shipping, machinery, to take but three of the most characteristic industries of the Palatinate, must inevitably be injured by any form of Protective tariff. Cotton, the greatest of all, must be injured the most of all. Cheapness of production is vital to cotton, because cotton is mainly an export trade and largely a trade concerned with serving Oriental markets — China and India — where a very small rise in the price of the finished article means not merely an advantage to competitors, but a great shrinkage in the consuming power of the population who purchase from you.

The effect of a tariff upon trade in Lancashire. Lancashire has nothing to gain because the cotton trade is already supreme; it holds the home market practically without intrusion; it overleaps the tariffs even of the countries where the raw cotton is grown; and it easily maintains its primacy in every foreign and in every neutral market. You have nothing to gain; you have everything to lose. Any increase in the cost of manufacture must reduce the margin of profit of the cotton spinner, any increase in the cost of living must affect the wages of the cotton operative. If either of these two evils should result the consequence will follow in labour troubles, and nobody knows better than you how perilous to the permanent interests of the cotton trade, how disastrous to the actual, current, day-to-day life of Manchester these disturbances and disputes between employers and operatives are. And yet I am positive that in the process of adjusting the new burden which the Tariff Reform party seek to put upon you there could not fail to be deep and bitter quarrels between the mill-owners and the workers throughout the whole of Lancashire.

What are you going to do about India? And, lastly, what about India? We ask these questions again and again. No answer is ever offered to us in reply — only the same stale, old, stupid fallacies, the old catch-penny arguments and trick statistics are advanced as a substitute for a definite answer upon this great question. We must rule India justly. We must give to the people of India the fiscal system which we honourably believe is the best for their interests. We honestly believe that Free Trade is best for their interests. We believe it is best for our interests, too, and we practise what we preach. But if we come to the conclusion by a majority in this country that Free Trade is wrong, that nations can get richer by excluding the foreign goods they want to buy, then be sure that that argument holds good for India too. Then be sure you will not be able to deny to India the right to protect herself against the severe competition of Lancashire, and the countervailing excise duties which exist in India at the present moment could not, I believe, be maintained for a year after Great Britain herself had adopted a Protective system.

The instance of machinery. I have dealt with cotton. Let me say a word about machinery. Our foreign trade in machinery of all kinds is a very valuable, lucrative, progressive feature in our exports. A supply of cheap iron and steel is essential to the development and prosperity of that trade. I see that

Mr Balfour in his manifesto promises that Tariff Reform will secure this country from unfair competition in the home market. The greatest amount of unfair competition in the home market is the unfair competition of one Englishman against another. But as to the competition, the unfair competition as it is called, which is directed upon this country from the outside, I presume that Mr Balfour means, among other things, that he would try to shut out the cheap steel which is sent into this country.

An illustration from steel. How he is going to shut it out he does not tell us, and it is quite clear that no tariff which has yet been talked of in this country would be of any use, because what is called 'dumped' steel, which is sent here as bankrupt stock, which is sent to be thrown down on the market at almost any price, would obviously not be prevented from coming in by the mere imposition of a ten per cent duty. But let us assume that Mr Balfour had a plan, and that he were able to exclude steel which he thought was likely to reach British manufacturers too cheap. Supposing that 10,000 tons of steel were coming here, and supposing Mr Balfour succeeded in shutting them out, what would happen? The 10,000 tons which were shut out from this country would then be for sale in the markets of the world. Where would they go? I conclude they would go elsewhere. They would go perhaps to Belgium, where the duties are low, or to the United States of America, which, in spite of all its great tariffs, buys cheap steel greedily when it gets the chance. But wherever they went they would go in competition with our own exports of steel, which are very large, and in successful competition, because if you could not compete with this dumped steel here in your own market, where it has to bear the cost of freight and insurance, how much less will you be able to compete with it in foreign or neutral markets, where you, equally with it, will be saddled with these charges.

The effect of shutting out cheap steel would be to the advantage of some foreign competitor. Therefore, the effect of shutting this cheap steel out would be to reduce British exports by exactly an equivalent amount. It would deprive your machinery manufacturers of all kinds in this country of the advantage of making a specially profitable bargain. It would transfer that advantage to some foreign competitor, and that foreign competitor would be strengthened by the possession of this cheap steel in his competition with you in the higher manufactures of steel, and practically of machinery. This is the notable plan for the improvement of British trade by putting a stop to unfair competition.

The happiness of millions depends upon the maintenance of Free Trade. I see before me a great, a splendid meeting of Manchester men. I see around me on the platform here high authorities in the cotton trade; I see in this hall the men who have it in their power — I firmly believe it — to make the decision of this great city. Let them remember how awful are their responsibilities. Here we are, a community of millions crowded together upon a soil which in this country would not support one-tenth, or, perhaps, one-twentieth of the number, raised to a high level of civilization, with all sorts of opportunities thrown open to our enterprise, but dependent absolutely for the foundations of our prosperity upon the operations which take place in the markets at one end of the world and the crops which ripen each year at another; dependent absolutely upon the free imports of food and raw material and upon the free and unfettered use of our intellect and enterprise to buy where we like in the markets of the whole world. On the maintenance of these simple truths depends the happiness of millions of families.

Foreign investments are not injurious to the mass of the people. I turn over in my mind the arguments of our opponents, and I hardly see one which has not been answered a hundred times. I hardly see one, the cheap and taking fallacy of which has not been seen through by every man who has gazed at it with a penetrating eye. I will take only one tonight to deal with, the argument that Free Trade has driven capital out of the country, and that the process of foreign investments is injurious to the mass of the British people. I take it because it is one of the most difficult, and because it is one of the most misleading forms in which the smashed-up arguments of Tariff Reform are put forward. Free Trade has driven capital out of the country. No, I beg pardon. Six months ago it was Free Trade. Now it is the Budget. I will make six statements on the subject of foreign investments, not one of which can be challenged.

Investment abroad is profitable. First, the process of investment abroad is profitable and it has been going on a long time. It is common to all rich and highly developed countries whatever their fiscal policy may be. It is calculated that Great Britain has invested three thousand millions sterling abroad on which she receives a not insignificant return of over a hundred and twenty millions sterling per annum. But Germany, that paradise of our would-be Protectionists, has succeeded already, though her industrial position is much more newly established than ours, in investing fifteen hundred millions of capital abroad. And France, it is calculated, has invested sixteen hundred millions. Even the United States of America, although they are greatly in debt to Europe, although they are buying back their securities as fast as they can, particularly their railway securities, and although they are still in the development stage — even the United States, by the working of circumstances which are

common to all modern nations, irrespective of their fiscal
system, have been induced to make large foreign investments. That is my first statement.

**Periods of rapid investment abroad have been periods of
most active development at home.** Secondly, I submit to you
as a fact which cannot be challenged that periods of very
rapid investment abroad have also been periods of the
most active development at home. That was true of the
period from 1887 to 1890; it was also true of the last period
for which we have completed records, the years 1907 and
1908, when you had most active investments abroad and a
record production in exports and manufacture at home.

Overseas investments have developed the British Empire.
Thirdly, I say that British overseas investments have developed the British Empire. Fully a half of the whole of the
capital we have invested abroad has been invested in India
and in other British possessions. You in Lancashire know
how important it is to your trade that India and British
possessions should be prosperous and developing.

Scarcely any British money invested in competing industries.
Fourthly, it is a very curious thing that scarcely any British
money has been invested in enterprises which compete with
industries of the United Kingdom and nearly all of our great
volume of foreign investments has gone to developing areas
whence we draw supplies of food and raw material.

Foreign investments stimulate British trade. Fifthly, the
capital which is invested abroad goes out almost entirely in
the form of British exports, thus stimulating British trade.

The interest comes home in food and raw materials. Sixthly,
the interest on these investments due to us comes home in

the form of food and raw materials. Without these supplies of food and raw materials we could not carry on our world-wide business for a twelvemonth.

British industry is not suffering from lack of capital. There is no evidence at all meanwhile that British industry suffers from lack of capital. Why, ever since the Budget there has been no rush to sell British stocks. The prices at which the leading British municipal and industrial securities stand compare favourably not merely with foreign industrial and municipal investments, but with the great national stocks of some of the most powerful nations in Europe.

Why, the credit of Manchester — after the Budget — is superior to the credit of the German Empire. Manchester Corporation 'threes' are at ninety-one, and German 'threes' at eighty-four — under Free Trade — after the Budget. And the credit of Liverpool is superior to that of Italy — after the Budget. Trade is brisk, and I am glad to say (speaking as one who has some opportunity of hearing these little things) that there are indications of an ever-strengthening revival in the general trade of the country.

The monthly accounts show that the United Kingdom exports for November have increased by £4,174,040 over the corresponding exports of November, 1908 — £4,174,040 in one month — after the Budget.

Is it difficult to obtain money 'even for the best British enterprises'? Lord Rothschild said in the House of Lords, 'It is difficult, if not impossible, to obtain money even for the best English enterprises.' Well now, in the last four years no less than fifteen millions sterling has been forthcoming for investment in new cotton-spinning and weaving sheds in Lancashire alone — sheds and mills which it is calculated are capable of providing employment for 55,000 additional operatives. We have added more spindles to our cotton mills than the whole cotton trade of Germany possesses. And this expansion of the staple industry of Lancashire has produced a certain increase in numerous smaller allied industries dependent thereupon.

The danger is too rapid development. Indeed, the only complaint which I have heard made on that subject is not the scarcity of enterprises and capital, but the tendency to over-investment and over-construction, which has led to the erection of mills in Lancashire, sometimes on perhaps rather speculative finance, beyond the requirements of the trade and the present capacity of the cotton crop. Indeed, I remember having had to receive in the last two months a deputation at the Board of Trade, who waited upon me, much concerned at the too rapid development of mill construction in Lancashire disproportionate to the growth of the trade.

The case of the Suez Canal. Well, let me close this question of foreign investments by taking a concrete instance, and as I have the opportunity of picking it out for myself, naturally I pick out a good one. In the year 1879 or 1880, Lord Beaconsfield — the same Lord Beaconsfield who said Protection was not only dead but damned — Lord Beaconsfield made a foreign investment. He bought Suez Canal shares for £4,000,000 sterling. Well, that was a foreign investment; that was diverting capital from British labour to a foreign country; that was, according to Protectionist jargon, taking the bread out of the mouth of the British working man. That investment today is worth £20,000,000 at least, and we are drawing a revenue of £1,100,000 a year regularly, fresh and fresh every year, without lifting a finger, as a result of that fortunate investment abroad.

That is one foreign investment which does not seem to have been a very bad thing for the British people. But, of course, not all are so successful. There are losses as well as gains; and the return from the rest of our foreign investments is enjoyed by private people. That, I think, shows that among the investing classes there is a fair field for direct taxation, when the necessary requirements of the State have to be met. But the fact remains that foreign investment and its returns are a powerful stimulus to the industrial system of Great Britain, that they give to the capital of this country a share in the new wealth of the whole world which is gradually coming under the control of scientific development, and that they sensibly enlarge the resources on which the State can rely for peaceful development and war-like need.

How 'Tariff Reform' would affect the Manchester Ship Canal. You could not find a better object-lesson either for the defence of Free Trade or for the justification of land reform than the Manchester Ship Canal. Why, what is the Manchester Ship Canal? It is a channel to enable foreign goods to be imported cheaply into this country. It is a tube to bring dumping into the very heart of our national life. And you have built it; you have built this canal yourselves; you have built it at great cost; you have dragged the Trojan horse within your own walls yourselves. But more; you have thrived upon it. You have actually got fat in the process of committing this extraordinary folly. The Manchester Ship Canal has been an enormous stimulus to the trade and prosperity of Manchester and of Lancashire as a whole. Nobody denies it; nobody can deny it.

And what kind of fools are those who come to us and say that when we have spent so much money to build the Canal to make foreign goods cheap in the Manchester market, we should spend more money on Custom-house officers and

Custom-house buildings in order to make them dear again?
The arguments are not only against reason and logic — they
are against nature.

The free waterway is vital. The free waterway of the Canal
is vital to Manchester. You might as well throttle the air-
pipe of a submarine diver, in order to protect him from the
draught, as choke your Ship Canal with a Protective tariff.
It is worth while, I think, that those who are interested in
the Canal should observe that Mr Wyndham at Liverpool
proposed to tax timber, and Mr Chaplin in Manchester declared that he would tax corn. As for Mr Balfour, he is a
leader who does whatever his followers tell him — only,
when he knows his followers are wrong, he does it half-
heartedly. Well, now, timber is almost as important an
item in the freights of the Canal as cotton, and grain is more
than twice as important in the freights of the Canal as
cotton. Both timber and grain are to be struck at by the
Tariff Reformer, and so all concerned in the prosperity of the
Ship Canal should take due notice. Let the shareholders, who
have not had too much out of it so far, let the Manchester
Corporation and the ratepayers of Manchester take notice,
and let the dockers, the men who unload the ships at the
wharves, take notice of the amiable project which is in con-
templation against their interests in the traffic and activity
of the Manchester Ship Canal.

**Why should Mr Balfour exempt cotton if he taxes other com-
modities?** Mr Balfour has told us that he is going to exempt
cotton. We must be thankful for small mercies; but I want
to ask a question. Why should he exempt cotton? On what
grounds? Surely scientific taxation is not going to descend
to electioneering. If the foreigner will pay the duty on
timber and on grain, why won't he make a good job of it and

pay it on cotton, too? If these articles have the faculty of
not going up in the British market when they are taxed,
why should not cotton be made to come in on the same basis?
Why should not the cotton-grower of the United States, to
take a favourite argument of the Protectionist, be made to
'pay a toll' for bringing his cotton to our markets? If cotton
is to be exempted on the ground that it is the raw material
of manufacture, why is not grain to be exempted on the
ground that it is the raw material of human life?

What difference will it make to the cotton trade, if the
ultimate cost of production is increased, whether it is increased by taxes on the cotton that they spin or taxes on
the corn that they eat? The trade as a whole will have to
bear the loss and the different sections of the trade will have
to fight it out between them, who is to bear the larger share.
That being so, I foresee an avenue of disastrous consequences
from which anyone who loves this great and famous county
must desire to save it.

All these reflections rise from the consideration of that
noble work of British skill and enterprise that has brought
the sea to Manchester.

**The idea that we can 'make the foreigner pay' is a grotesque
absurdity and a cruel deception.** If I thought for one moment
that it was possible by a Protective tariff to eliminate unemployment, I assure you I would not be very long in
raising my voice in favour of that system. If I thought it
would be possible, even at some sacrifice to the whole community, to make sure that there was absolute security for all
the industrious bread-winners and all the workers of our land,
I agree that we might run great risks and make novel experi-
ments in order to achieve that end; and, of course, if I could
bring myself to believe for one moment that we could raise
the revenue to pay for our Dreadnoughts and for our Old-Age

Pensions by taxing the foreigner, I would set to work this very night. But, gentlemen, the idea that a nation can raise its revenue by taxing the foreigner, that you can defray the great purposes and expenses of the nation out of the coffers of foreign countries, is one of the most grotesque absurdities that ever entered into the brains of silly people, and is one of the most cruel deceptions that ever was exploited by knaves. It is no doubt true that by sudden and unexpected alterations under a tariff a nation may from time to time throw some of the burdens upon a foreign country, but the gains will be very small and transient, because the actual natural conditions of competition and bargaining between the countries must prevail, and these natural conditions are not altered by the imposition of a duty. And although for a moment you may force the foreign importer to pay a very small portion of the duty in certain exceptional cases, in the long run, and as soon as the market changes favourably to him, he is able to secure back all that you have taken from him; and in addition, no doubt, you lose through the disturbance and friction caused to the intercourse between the two countries.

One of the most absurd delusions of mankind. The idea that a great nation can raise its revenue from this source is among the most absurd delusions of mankind. I know those people who think they can coin the moonlight into silver and mint the sunshine into gold, are always running about with some of these plans for getting rich quickly and securing wealth without having to work for it. From my experience it seems a profound natural law which governs all our actions that you get nothing for nothing and precious little for twopence-halfpenny.

How is it that Germany borrows instead of 'taxing the foreigner'? If it were possible for nations to raise their revenue by taxing the foreigner, how is it that the Germans, now that they are face to face with a heavy deficit, should have to turn elsewhere to secure the necessary money, and have had to borrow until their credit has fallen below that of Italy? How is it that the Germans do not go on taxing the foreigner? And if we in this country have all these years been taxed by all the foreign countries in the world, and if, besides paying for our own Government and our own Navy — which are quite expensive enough — we have been supporting all these foreign countries, how is it we have not been ruined and crushed down to the ground under these stupendous burdens?

The average condition of the mass of our nation superior to that of any other country in Europe. After all, there are only forty-five million of us, and even with the great advantage of being ruled by the House of Lords, it seems to me difficult to suppose that we could have easily sustained the whole burden of our own administration, and paid such large contributions to our foreign friends. And, at the end of the process, after sixty years of being ruined by Free Trade, it is an undoubted fact that, notwithstanding all the evils which we see in the social life of our country, the average condition of the mass of the nation is superior to that attained by the masses of the people in any other country in Europe. The anxiety, suffering, and insecurity which prey upon the underside of the labour market is a cruel and shocking fact, and it is one of the very first subjects which demands, and is receiving, the attention of the Government of the country. But it is absolutely true to say that the condition of the working classes of Great Britain as a whole is superior to the condition of the working classes of Germany. I believe that to be an unanswerable fact, and I believe the Germans think so, too.

Tariff Reform would make the British Empire odious to the working people. I am quite prepared to prove to you that Protection or Tariff Reform, call it which they will, would be injurious to the whole country; that it would cripple our export trade; that it would affect the consuming power of our home market; that it would raise prices in the home market to the restriction of enterprise and to the hardship of the poor; that it would create an enormous new crop of vested interests like the liquor trade at the present time, with which the widow and the orphan would soon become entangled, and from which you would never shake yourselves free; that it would lead to the formation of trusts and corners; that it would certainly conduce, as it does in so many countries, to the corruption of politics and politicians; that, so far as our relations with foreign countries are concerned, it would disturb the course of trade, and it would aggravate that instability among different States and countries from which already we suffer and for which already we pay so heavy a toll in national defence; and, lastly, that if it included the preferential taxation of food for the sake of uniting the British Empire it would, in the words of a great man now unhappily disabled from taking his share in the conflict — it would 'make the British Empire odious to the working people.'

THE PEOPLE'S LAND

4 THE PEOPLE'S LAND

The best way to make private property secure and respected is to bring the processes by which it is gained into harmony with the general interests of the public. We are often assured by sagacious persons that the civilization of modern States is largely based upon respect for the rights of private property. If that be true, it is also true to say that that respect cannot be secured, and ought not, indeed, to be expected, unless property is associated in the minds of the great mass of the people with ideas of justice and of reason.

It is, therefore, of the first importance to the country — to any country — that there should be vigilant and persistent efforts to prevent abuses, to distribute the public burdens fairly among all classes, and to establish good laws governing the methods by which wealth may be acquired. The best way to make private property secure and respected is to bring the processes by which it is gained into harmony with the general interests of the public. When and where property is associated with the idea of reward for services rendered, with the idea of reward for high gifts and special aptitudes displayed or for faithful labour done, then property will be honoured. When it is associated with processes which are beneficial, or which at the worst are not actually injurious to the commonwealth, then property will be unmolested; but when it is associated with ideas of wrong and of unfairness, with processes of restriction and monopoly, and other forms of injury to the community, then I think that you will find that property will be assailed and will be endangered.

Land differs from all other forms of property. It is quite true that the land monopoly is not the only monopoly which exists, but it is by far the greatest of monopolies — it is a perpetual monopoly, and it is the mother of all other forms of monopoly. It is quite true that unearned increments in land are not the only form of unearned or undeserved profit which individuals are able to secure; but it is the principal form of unearned increment which is derived from processes which are not merely not beneficial, but which are positively detrimental to the general public. Land, which is a necessity of human existence, which is the original source of all wealth, which is strictly limited in extent, which is fixed in geographical position — land, I say, differs from all other forms of property in these primary and fundamental conditions. Nothing is more amusing than to watch the efforts of our monopolist opponents to prove that other forms of property and increment are exactly the same and are similar in all respects to the unearned increment in land. They talk to us of the increased profits of a doctor or a lawyer from the growth of population in the towns in which they live. They talk to us of the profits of a railway through a greater degree of wealth and activity in the districts through which it runs. They tell us of the profits which are derived from a rise in stocks and shares, and even of those which are sometimes derived from the sale of pictures and works of art, and they ask us, as if it were the only complaint, 'Ought not all these other forms to be taxed too?'

Misleading analogies. But see how misleading and false all these analogies are. The windfalls which people with artistic gifts are able from time to time to derive from the sale of a picture — from a Vandyke or a Holbein — may here and there be very considerable. But pictures do not get in anybody's way. They do not lay a toll on anybody's labour; they do not touch enterprise and production at any point; they do not affect any of the creative processes upon which the material well-being of millions depends; and if a rise in stocks and shares confers profits on the fortunate holders far beyond what they expected, or indeed, deserved, nevertheless, that profit has not been reaped by withholding from the community the land which it needs, but, on the contrary, apart from mere gambling, it has been reaped by supplying industry with the capital without which it could not be carried on. If the railway makes greater profits, it is usually because it carries more goods and more passengers. If a doctor or a lawyer enjoys a better practice, it is because the doctor attends more patients and more exacting patients, and because the lawyer pleads more suits in the courts and more important suits. At every stage the doctor or the lawyer is giving service in return for his fees, and if the service is too poor or the fees are too high, other doctors and other lawyers can come freely into competition. There is constant service, there is constant competition; there is no monopoly, there is no injury to the public interest, there is no impediment to the general progress.

Unearned increment. Fancy comparing these healthy processes with the enrichment which comes to the landlord who happens to own a plot of land on the outskirts or at the centre of one of our great cities, who watches the busy population around him making the city larger, richer, more convenient, more famous every day, and all the while sits still and does nothing. Roads are made, streets are made, railway services are improved, electric light turns night into day, electric trams glide swiftly to and fro, water is brought from reservoirs a hundred miles off in the mountains — and all the while the landlord sits still. Every one of those improvements is effected by the labour and at the cost of other people. Many of the most important are effected at the cost of the municipality and of the ratepayers. To not one of those improvements does the land monopolist as a land monopolist contribute, and yet by every one of them the value of his land is sensibly enhanced. He renders no service to the community, he contributes nothing to the general welfare; he contributes nothing even to the process from which his own enrichment is derived. If the land were occupied by shops or by dwellings, the municipality at least would secure the rates upon them in aid of the general fund, but the land may be unoccupied, undeveloped, it may be what is called 'ripening' — ripening at the expense of the whole city, of the whole country, for the unearned increment of its owner. Roads perhaps may have to be diverted to avoid this forbidden area. The merchant going to his office, the artisan going to his work, have to make a detour or pay a tram fare to avoid it. The citizens are losing their chance of developing the land, the city is losing its rates, the State is losing its taxes which would have accrued if the natural development had taken place; and that share has to be replaced at the expense of the other ratepayers and taxpayers, and the nation as a whole is losing in the competition of the world — the hard and growing competition of the world — both in time and money. And all the while the land monopolist has only to sit still and watch complacently his property multiplying in value, sometimes manifold, without either effort or contribution on his part; and that is justice!

Unearned increment reaped in exact proportion to the disservice done. But let us follow the process a little further,

The population of the city grows and grows still larger year by year, the congestion in the poorer quarters becomes acute, rents and rates rise hand in hand, and thousands of families are crowded into one-roomed tenements. There are 120,000 persons living in one-roomed tenements in Glasgow alone at the present time. At last the land becomes ripe for sale — that means that the price is too tempting to be resisted any longer — and then, and not till then, it is sold by the yard or by the inch at ten times, or twenty times, or even fifty times, its agricultural value, on which alone hitherto it has been rated for the public service. The greater the population around the land, the greater the injury which they have sustained by its protracted denial, the more inconvenience which has been caused to everybody, the more serious the loss in economic strength and activity, the larger will be the profit of the landlord when the sale is finally accomplished. In fact, you may say that the unearned increment on the land is on all fours with the profit gathered by one of those American speculators who engineer a corner in corn, or meat, or cotton, or some other vital commodity, and that the unearned increment in land is reaped by the land monopolist in exact proportion, not to the service but to the disservice done.

The drag on enterprise. It is monopoly which is the keynote, and where monopoly prevails, the greater the injury to society the greater the reward of the monopolist will be. See how all this evil process strikes at every form of industrial activity. The municipality, wishing for broader streets, better houses, more healthy, decent, scientifically planned towns, is made to pay, and is made to pay in exact proportion, or to a very great extent in proportion, as it has exerted itself in the past to make improvements. The more it has improved the town, the more it has increased the land value, and the more it will have to pay for any land it may wish to acquire. The manufacturer purposing to start a new industry, proposing to erect a great factory offering employment to thousands of hands, is made to pay such a price for his land that the purchase price hangs round the neck of his whole business, hampering his competitive power in every market, clogging him far more than any foreign tariff in his export competition, and the land values strike down through the profits of the manufacturer on to the wages of the workman. The railway company wishing to build a new line finds that the price of land which yesterday was only rated at agricultural value has risen to a prohibitive figure the moment it was known that the new line was projected, and either the railway is not built or, if it is, is built only on terms which largely transfer to the landowner the profits which are due to the shareholders and the advantages which should have accrued to the travelling public.

Every form of enterprise only undertaken after the land monopolist has skimmed the cream off for himself. It does not matter where you look or what examples you select, you will see that every form of enterprise, every step in material progress, is only undertaken after the land monopolist has skimmed the cream off for himself, and everywhere today the man or the public body who wishes to put land to its highest use is forced to pay a preliminary fine in land values to the man who is putting it to an inferior use, and in some cases to no use at all. All comes back to the land value, and its owner for the time being is able to levy his toll upon all other forms of wealth and upon every form of industry. A portion, in some cases the whole, of every benefit which is laboriously acquired by the community is represented in the land value, and finds its way automatically into the landlord's pocket. If there is a rise in wages, rents are able to move forward, because the workers can afford to pay a little more. If the opening of a new railway or a new tramway or the institution of an improved service of workmen's trains or a lowering of fares or a new invention or any other public convenience affords a benefit to the workers in any particular district, it becomes easier for them to live, and therefore the landlord and the ground landlord, one on top of the other, are able to charge them more for the privilege of living there.

The landowner absorbs a share of almost every public and private benefit. Some years ago in London there was a tollbar on a bridge across the Thames, and all the working people who lived on the south side of the river had to pay a daily toll of one penny for going and returning from their work. The spectacle of these poor people thus mulcted on so large a proportion of their earnings appealed to the public conscience, an agitation was set on foot, municipal authorities were roused, and at the cost of the ratepayers the bridge was freed and the toll removed. All those people who used the bridge were saved sixpence a week. Within a very short period from that time the rents on the south side of the river were found to have advanced by about sixpence a week, or the amount of the toll which had been remitted. And a friend of mine was telling me the other day that in the parish of Southwark about £350 a year, roughly speaking, was given away in doles of bread by charitable people in connection with one of the churches, and as a consequence of this the competition for small houses, but more particularly for single-roomed tenements, is, we are told, so great that rents are considerably higher than in the neighbouring district. All goes back to the land, and the landowner, who in many cases, in most cases, is a worthy person utterly unconscious of the character of the methods by which he is enriched, is enabled with resistless strength to absorb to himself a share of almost every public and every private benefit, however important or however pitiful those benefits may be.

The Manchester Ship Canal and unearned increments. Now let the Manchester Ship Canal tell its tale about the land. It has a story to tell which is just as simple and just as pregnant as its story about Free Trade. When it was resolved to build the Canal, the first thing that had to be done was to buy the land. Before the resolution to build the Canal was taken, the land on which the Canal flows — or perhaps I should say 'stands' — was, in the main, agricultural land, paying rates on an assessment from 30s. to £2 an acre. I am told that 4,495 acres of land purchased fell within that description out of something under 5,000 purchased altogether. Immediately after the decision, the 4,495 acres were sold for £777,000 sterling — or an average of £172 an acre — that is to say, five or six times the agricultural value of the land and the value on which it had been rated for public purposes.

Now what had the landowner done for the community; what enterprise had he shown; what service had he rendered; what capital had he risked in order that he should gain this enormous multiplication of the value of his property? I will tell you in one word what he had done. Can you guess it? Nothing.

But it was not only the owners of the land that was needed for making the Canal, who were automatically enriched. All the surrounding land either having a frontage on the Canal or access to it rose and rose rapidly, and splendidly, in value. By the stroke of a fairy wand, without toil, without risk, without even a half-hour's thought many landowners in Salford, Eccles, Stretford, Irlam, Warrington, Runcorn, etc., found themselves in possession of property which had trebled, quadrupled, quintupled in value.

Apart from the high prices which were paid, there was a heavy bill for compensation, severance, disturbance, and injurious affection where no land was taken — injurious affection, namely, raising the land not taken many times in value — all this was added to the dead-weight cost of construction. All this was a burden on those whose labour, skill, and capital created this great public work. Much of this land today is still rated at ordinary agricultural value, and in order to make sure that no injustice is done, in order to make quite certain that these landowners are not injured by our system of government, half their rates are, under the Agricultural Rates Act, paid back to them. The balance is made up by you. The land is still rising in value, and with every day's work that every man in this neighbourhood does and with every addition to the prosperity of Manchester and improvement of this great city, the land is further enhanced in value.

The shareholders and the ratepayers. I have told you what happened to the landowners. Let us see what happened to the shareholders and the ratepayers who found the money. The ordinary shareholders, who subscribed eight millions, have had no dividend yet. The Corporation loan of five millions, interest on which is borne on the rates each year, had, until 1907, no return upon its capital. A return has come at last, and no doubt the future prospects are good; but there was a long interval — even for the corporation. These are the men who did the work. These are the men who put up the money. I want to ask you a question. Do you think it would be very unfair if the owners of all this automatically created land value due to the growth of the city, to the enterprise of the community, and to the sacrifices made by the shareholders — do you think it would have been very unfair, if they had been made to pay a proportion, at any rate, of the unearned increment which they secured, back to the city and the community?

The system to be attacked, not individuals. I hope you will understand that when I speak of the land monopolist I am dealing more with the process than with the individual land-owner. I have no wish to hold any class up to public disapprobation. I do not think that the man who makes money by unearned increment in land is morally a worse man than anyone else who gathers his profit where he finds it in this hard world under the law and according to common usage. It is not the individual I attack, it is the system. It is not the man who is bad, it is the law which is bad. It is not the man who is blameworthy for doing what the law allows and what other men do; it is the State which would be blameworthy were it not to endeavour to reform the law and correct the practice. We do not want to punish the landlord. We want to alter the law.

We do not go back on the past. Look at our actual proposal. We do not go back on the past. We accept as our basis the value as it stands today. The tax on the increment of land begins by recognizing and franking the past increment. We look only to the future, and for the future we say only this, that the community shall be the partner in any further increment above the present value after all the owner's improvements have been deducted. We say that the State and the municipality should jointly levy a toll upon the future unearned increment of the land. The toll of what? Of the whole? No. Of a half? No. Of a quarter? No. Of a fifth — that is the proposal of the Budget, and that is robbery, that is plunder, that is communism and spoliation, that is the social revolution at last, that is the overturn of civilized society, that is the end of the world foretold in the Apocalypse! Such is the increment tax about which so much chatter and outcry are raised at the present time, and upon which I will say that no more fair, considerate, or salutary proposal for taxation has ever been made in the House of Commons.

Tax on capital value of undeveloped land. But there is another proposal concerning land values which is not less important. I mean the tax on the capital value of undeveloped urban or suburban land. The income derived from land and its rate-able value under the present law depend upon the use to which the land is put, consequently income and rateable value are not always true or complete measures of the value of the land. Take the case to which I have already referred of the man who keeps a large plot in or near a growing town idle for years while it is ripening — that is to say, while it is rising in price through the exertions of the surrounding community and the need of that community for more room to live. Take that case. I daresay you have formed your own opinion upon it. Mr Balfour, Lord Lansdowne, and the Conservative Party generally, think that that is an admirable arrangement. They speak of the profits of the land monopolist as if they were the fruits of thrift and industry and a pleasing example for the poorer classes to imitate. We do not take that view of the process. We think it is a dog-in-the-manger game. We see the evil, we see the imposture upon the public, and we see the consequences in crowded slums, in hampered commerce, in distorted or restricted development, and in congested centres of population, and we say here and now to the land monopolist who is holding up his land — and the pity is it was not said before — you shall judge for yourselves whether it is a fair offer or not. We say to the land monopolist: 'This property of yours might be put to immediate use with general advantage. It is at this minute saleable in the market at ten times the value at which it is rated. If you choose to keep it idle in the expectation of still further unearned increment, then at least you shall be taxed at the true selling value in the meanwhile.' And the Budget proposes a tax of a halfpenny in the pound on the capital value of all such land; that is to say, a tax which is a little less in equivalent than the income tax would be upon the property if the property were fully developed. That is the second main proposal of the Budget with regard to the land, and its effects will be, first, to raise an expanding revenue for the needs of the State; secondly, half the proceeds of this tax, as well as of the other land taxes, will go to the municipalities and local authorities generally to relieve rates; thirdly, the effect will be, as we believe, to bring land into the market, and thus somewhat cheapen the price at which land is obtainable for every object, public and private, and by so doing we shall liberate new springs of enterprise and industry, we shall stimulate building, relieve overcrowding, and promote employment.

Nothing new in the principle of valuation for taxation. These two taxes, both in themselves financially, economically, and socially sound, carry with them a further notable advantage. We shall obtain a complete valuation of the whole of the land in the United Kingdom. We shall procure an up-to-date Domesday Book showing the capital value, apart from buildings and improvements, of every piece of land. Now, there is nothing new in the principle of valuation for taxation purposes. It was established fifteen years ago in Lord Rosebery's Government by the Finance Act of 1894, and it has been applied ever since without friction or inconvenience by Conservative administrations. And if there is nothing new in the principle of valuation, still less is there

anything new or unexpected in the general principles underlying the land proposals of the Budget. Why, Lord Rosebery
declared himself in favour of taxation of land values fifteen
years ago. Lord Balfour has said a very great many shrewd
and sensible things on this subject which he is, no doubt,
very anxious to have overlooked at the present time. The
House of Commons has repeatedly affirmed the principle,
not only under Liberal Governments, but — which is much
more remarkable — under a Conservative Government.
Four times during the last Parliament Mr Trevelyan's Bill
for the taxation of land values was brought before the House
of Commons and fully discussed, and twice it was read a
second time during the last Parliament with its great Conservative majority, the second time by a majority of no less
than ninety votes. The House of Lords, in adopting Lord
Camperdown's amendment to the Scottish Valuation Bill,
has absolutely conceded the principle of rating undeveloped
land upon its selling value, although it took very good care
not to apply the principle; and all the greatest municipal
corporations in England and Scotland — many of them over-
whelmingly Conservative in complexion — have declared
themselves in favour of the taxation of land values, and,
after at least a generation of study, examination, and debate,
the time has come when we should take the first step to put
these principles into practical effect.

The exemption of agricultural land from taxation. It is said
that the land taxes fall too heavily upon the agricultural
landowner and the country gentleman. There could be no
grosser misrepresentation of the Budget. Few greater dis-
services can be done to the agricultural landowner, whose
property has in the last thirty years in many cases declined
in value, than to confuse him with the ground landlord in a
great city, who has netted enormous sums through the

growth and the needs of the population of the city. None of the new land taxes touch agricultural land, while it remains agricultural land. No cost of the system of valuation which we are going to carry into effect will fall at all upon the individual owner of landed property. He will not be burdened in any way by these proposals. On the contrary, now that an amendment has been accepted permitting death duties to be paid in land in certain circumstances, the owner of a landed estate, instead of encumbering his estate by raising the money to pay off the death duties, can cut a portion from his estate; and this in many cases will be a sensible relief.

The concession to agricultural landowners. Secondly, we have given to agricultural landowners a substantial concession in regard to the deductions which they are permitted to make from income-tax assessment on account of the money which they spend as good landlords upon the upkeep of their properties, and we have raised the limit of deduction from twelve and a half per cent to twenty-five per cent.

The maligned Development Bill. Thirdly, there is the Development Act, which will help all the countryside and all classes of agriculturists, and which will help the landlord in the country among the rest. So much for that charge.

In no great country in the new world or the old have the working people yet secured the double advantage of Free Trade and Free Land together. Every nation in the world has its own way of doing things, its own successes and its own failures. All over Europe we see systems of land tenure which economically, socially, and politically are far superior to ours; but the benefits that those countries derive from their improved land systems are largely swept away, or at

E

any rate neutralized, by grinding tariffs on the necessaries of life and the materials of manufacture. In this country we have long enjoyed the blessings of Free Trade and of untaxed bread and meat, but against these inestimable benefits we have the evils of an unreformed and vicious land system. In no great country in the new world or the old have the working people yet secured the double advantage of Free Trade and Free Land together, by which I mean a commercial system and a land system from which, so far as possible, all forms of monopoly have been rigorously excluded. Sixty years ago our system of national taxation was effectively reformed, and immense and undisputed advantages accrued therefrom to all classes, the richest as well as the poorest. The system of local taxation today is just as vicious and wasteful, just as great an impediment to enterprise and progress, just as harsh a burden upon the poor, as the thousand taxes and Corn Law sliding scales of the 'hungry 'forties'. We are met in an hour of tremendous opportunity. 'You who shall liberate the land,' said Mr Cobden, 'will do more for your country than we have done in the liberation of its commerce.'

THE PEOPLE'S WELFARE

5 THE PEOPLE'S WELFARE

The British people more than any other people a manufacturing people. There is no evidence that the population of Great Britain has increased beyond the means of subsistence. On the contrary, our wealth is increasing faster than our numbers. Production is active; industry grows, and grows with astonishing vigour and rapidity. Enterprise in this country requires no artificial stimulant; if it errs at all, it is from time to time upon the side of over-trading and over-production. There is no ground for believing that this country is not capable of supporting an increasing population in a condition of expanding prosperity.

It must, however, be remembered that the British people are more than any other people in the world a manufacturing people. It is certain that our population could never have attained its present vast numbers, nor our country have achieved its position in the world, without an altogether unusual reliance upon manufacture as opposed to simple agriculture. The ordinary changes and transitions inseparable from the active life and growth of modern industry, therefore, operate here with greater relative intensity than in other countries. An industrial disturbance is more serious in Great Britain than in other countries, for it affects a far larger proportion of the people, and in their distresses the urban democracy are not sustained by the same solid backing of country folk and peasant cultivators that we see in other lands. It has, therefore, become a paramount necessity for us to make scientific provision against the fluctuations and set-backs which are inevitable in world commerce and in national industry.

The causes of unemployment. Disturbances of our industrial system are often started from outside this country by causes utterly beyond our control. When there is an epidemic of cholera, or typhoid, or diphtheria, a healthy person runs less risk than one whose constitution is prepared to receive the microbes of disease, and even if himself struck down, he stands a far greater chance of making a speedy recovery. The social and industrial conditions in Great Britain at this present time cannot be described as healthy. I discern in the present industrial system of our country three vicious conditions which make us peculiarly susceptible to any outside disturbance of international trade.

I. Lack of regulating machinery. First, the lack of any central organization of industry, or any general and concerted control either of ordinary Government work, or of any extraordinary relief works.

It would be possible for the Board of Trade to foretell with a certain amount of accuracy the degree of unemployment likely to be reached in any winter. It ought to be possible for some authority in some Government office — which I do not care — to view the whole situation in advance, and within certain limits to exert a powerful influence over the general distribution of Government contracts.

There is nothing economically unsound in increasing temporarily and artificially the demand for labour during a period of temporary and artificial contraction. There is a plain need of some averaging machinery to regulate and even-up the general course of the labour market, in the same way as the Bank of England, by its bank rate, regulates and corrects the flow of business enterprise. When the extent of the depression is foreseen, the extent of the relief should also be determined. There ought to be in permanent existence certain recognized industries of a useful, but uncompetitive character, like, we will say, afforestation, managed by public departments, and capable of being expanded or contracted according to the needs of the labour market, just as easily as you can pull out the stops or work the pedals of an organ.

In this way, you would not eliminate unemployment, you certainly would not prevent the creation of unemployables; but you would considerably limit the scale of unemployment, you would reduce the oscillation of the industrial system, you would increase its stability, and by every step that you took in that direction you would free thousands of your fellow-countrymen from undeserved agony and ruin, and a far greater number from the haunting dread of ruin. That is the first point — a gap, a hiatus in our social organization — to which I direct your attention tonight, and upon which the intelligence of this country ought to be concentrated.

II. The evil of casual labour. The second vicious condition is positive and not negative. I mean the gross, and, I sometimes fear, increasing evil of casual labour. We talk a great deal about the unemployed, but the evil of the *underemployed* is the tap-root of unemployment. There is a tendency in many trades, almost in all trades, to have a fringe of casual labour on hand, available as a surplus whenever there is a boom, flung back into the pool whenever there is a slump.

Employers and foremen in many trades are drawn consciously or unconsciously to distribute their work among a larger number of men than they regularly require, because this obviously increases their bargaining power with them, and supplies a convenient reserve for periods of brisk business activity.

And what I desire to impress upon you, and through you upon this country, is that the casual unskilled labourer who is habitually under-employed, who is lucky to get three, or at the outside four, days' work in the week, who may often be out of a job for three or four weeks at a time, who in bad times goes under altogether, and who in good times has no hope of security and no incentive to thrift, whose whole life and the lives of his wife and children are embarked in a sort of blind, desperate, fatalistic gamble with circumstances beyond his comprehension or control, that this poor man, this terrible and pathetic figure, is not as a class the result of accident or chance, is not casual because he wishes to be casual, is not casual as the consequence of some temporary disturbance soon put right. No; the casual labourer is here because he is wanted here. He is here in answer to a perfectly well-defined demand.

He is here as the result of economic causes which have been too long unregulated. He is not the natural product, he is an article manufactured, called into being, to suit the requirements, in the Prime Minister's telling phrase, of all industries at particular times and of particular industries at all times.

I suppose no department has more means of learning about these things than the Board of Trade, which is in friendly touch at every stage all over the country both with capital and labour. I publish that fact deliberately. I invite you to consider it, I want it to soak in. It appears to me that measures to check the growth and diminish the quantity of casual labour must be an essential part of any thorough or scientific attempt to deal with unemployment, and I would not proclaim this evil to you without having reason to believe that practicable means exist by which it can be greatly diminished.

III. Conditions of boy labour. If the first vicious condition which I have mentioned to you is lack of industrial organization, if the second is the evil of casual labour, there is a third not less important. I mean the present conditions of boy labour. The whole underside of the labour market is deranged by the competition of boys or young persons who do men's work for boys' wages, and are turned off so soon as they demand men's wages for themselves. That is the evil so far as it affects the men; but how does it affect the boys, the youth of our country, the heirs of all our exertion, the inheritors of that long treasure of history and romance, of science and knowledge — aye, of national glory, for which so many valiant generations have fought and toiled — the youth of Britain, how are we treating them in the twentieth century of the Christian era? Are they not being exploited? Are they not being demoralized? Are they not being thrown away?

Whereas the youth of the wealthier class is all kept under strict discipline until eighteen or nineteen, the mass of the nation runs wild after fourteen years of age. No doubt at first employment is easy to obtain. There is a wide and varied field; there are a hundred odd jobs for a lad; but almost every form of employment now open to young persons affords them no opening, is of no use to them whatever when they are grown up, and in a great number of cases the life which they lead is demoralizing and harmful. And what is the consequence? The consequence may be measured by this grim fact, that out of the unemployed applying for help under the Unemployed Workmen Act, no less than twenty-eight per cent are between twenty and

thirty years of age, that is to say, men in the first flush of
their strength and manhood already hopelessly adrift on
the dark and tumultuous ocean of life. Upon this subject,
I say to you deliberately that no boy or girl ought to be
treated merely as cheap labour, that up to eighteen years of
age every boy and girl in this country should, as in the old
days of apprenticeship, be learning a trade as well as earning
a living.

**The policy of the Budget is not a revolution, but a far-
reaching and complex scheme of social reform.** We live in
stirring times. We read a lot of history when we go to school.
A great thing is to recognize history when it really happens.
Everyone can recognize history when it has happened, but
the wise man knows at the moment what is vital and
permanent, what is lasting and memorable, and can pick it
out from the ordinary ebb and flow of political affairs. We
have entered upon a period of crisis and conflict more grave
and crucial than any living man has known, and it is a
conflict which I think has been more deliberately undertaken and will be more resolutely fought through by both
sides than any political conflict that we can recall. Terribly
important as economic and constitutional questions may be,
the fiscal system of a country and the system of Government which prevails in a country are only means to an end,
and that end must be to create conditions favourable to the
social and moral welfare of the masses of the citizens. I
think the course of public affairs during the last four years
must have been satisfactory to you. A new strength has
come into political life, and has filled it with a reality and a
seriousness which many were beginning to feel had departed
when Mr Gladstone died. We have left the wilderness of
phrases and formulas, the cut and dried party issues, and we
have broken violently into a world of constructive action. It

would be an exaggeration to speak of these changes as though they were a revolution. They are not a revolution, but, taken altogether, the policy which has been unfolded to this country during the last two or three years, and which is gripped together and carried forward by the Budget — that policy which the Lords have for the time being brought to a full stop — constitutes by far the largest, most scientific, most deliberate, most resolute attempt at social organization and social advance which any man living can remember.

Britain at the cross-ways. The social conditions of the British people in the early years of the twentieth century cannot be contemplated without deep anxiety. The anxiety is keen because it arises out of uncertainty. It is the gnawing anxiety of suspense. What is the destiny of our country to be? Nothing is settled either for or against us. We have no reason to despair; still less have we any reason to be self-satisfied. All is still in our hands for good or for ill. We have the power today to choose our fortune, and I believe there is no nation in the world, perhaps there never has been in history, any nation which at one and the same moment was confronted with such opposite possibilities, was threatened on the one hand by more melancholy disaster, and cheered on the other by more bright, yet not unreasonable hopes. The two roads are open. We are at the cross-ways. If we stand on in the old happy-go-lucky way, the richer classes ever growing in wealth and in number, and ever declining in responsibility, the very poor remaining plunged or plunging even deeper into helpless, hopeless misery, then I think there is nothing before us but savage strife between class and class, with an increasing disorganization, with an increasing destruction of human strength and human virtue — nothing, in fact, but that dual degeneration which comes from the simultaneous waste of extreme wealth and of extreme want.

The enemies of Britain. Now we have had over here lately colonial editors from all the colonies of the British Empire, and what is the opinion which they expressed as to the worst thing they saw in the old country? The representatives of every colony have expressed the opinion that the worst they saw here, was the extreme of poverty side by side with the extreme of luxury. Do not you think it is very impressive to find an opinion like that, expressed in all friendship and sincerity, by men of our own race who have come from lands which are so widely scattered over the surface of the earth, and are the product of such varied conditions? Is it not impressive to find that they are all agreed, coming as they do from Australia, or Canada, or South Africa, or New Zealand, that the greatest danger to the British Empire and to the British people is not to be found among the enormous fleets and armies of the European Continent, nor in the solemn problems of Hindustan; it is not the 'Yellow Peril' nor the 'Black Peril' nor any danger in the wide circuit of colonial and foreign affairs. No, it is here in our midst, close at home, close at hand in the vast growing cities of England and Scotland, and in the dwindling and cramped villages of our denuded countryside. It is there you will find the seeds of Imperial ruin and national decay — the unnatural gap between rich and poor, the divorce of the people from the land, the want of proper discipline and training in our youth, the exploitation of boy labour, the physical degeneration which seems to follow so swiftly on civilized poverty, the awful jumbles of an obsolete Poor Law, the horrid havoc of the liquor traffic, the constant insecurity in the means of subsistence and employment which breaks the heart of many a sober, hard-working man, the absence of any established minimum standard of life and comfort among the workers, and, at the other end, the swift increase of vulgar, joyless luxury — here are the enemies of Britain. Beware lest they shatter the foundations of her power.

The conflict. Then look at the other side, look at the forces for good, the moral forces, the spiritual forces, the civic, the scientific, the patriotic forces which make for order and harmony and health and life. Are they not tremendous too? Do we not see them everywhere, in every town, in every class, in every creed, strong forces worthy of Old England, coming to her rescue, fighting for her soul? That is the situation in our country as I see it this afternoon — two great armies evenly matched, locked in fierce conflict with each other all along the line, swaying backwards and forwards in strife — and for my part I am confident that the right will win, that the generous influences will triumph over the selfish influences, that the organizing forces will devour the forces of degeneration, and that the British people will emerge triumphant from their struggles to clear the road and lead the march amongst the foremost nations of the world.

On which side does the Budget count? Well, now, I want to ask you a question. I daresay there are some of you who do not like this or that particular point in the Budget, who do not like some particular argument or phrase which some of us may have used in advocating or defending it. But it is not of these details that I speak; the question I want each of you to ask himself is this: on which side of this great battle which I have described to you does the Budget count? Can any of you, looking at it broadly and as a whole, looking on the policy which surrounds it, and which depends upon it, looking at the arguments by which it is defended, as well as the arguments by which it is opposed — can any one doubt that the Budget in its essential character and meaning, in its spirit and in its practical effect, would be a tremendous reinforcement, almost like a new army coming up at the end of the day, upon the side of all those forces and influences which are fighting for the life and health and progress of our race?

Social organization. (i) National Insurance. Upon the Budget and upon the policy of the Budget depends a far-reaching plan of social organization designed to give a greater measure of security to all classes, but particularly to the labouring classes. In the centre of that plan stands the policy of National Insurance. The Chancellor of the Exchequer has been for more than a year at work upon this scheme, and it is proposed — I hope next year, if there is a next year — it is proposed, working through the great friendly societies, which have done so much in valuable work on these lines, to make sure that, by the aid of a substantial subvention from the State, even the poorest steady worker or the poorest family shall be enabled to make provision against sickness, against invalidity, and for the widows and orphans who may be left behind.

(ii) Unemployment Insurance. Side by side with this is the scheme of insurance against unemployment which I hope to have the honour of passing through Parliament next year. The details of that scheme are practically complete, and it will enable upwards of two and a quarter millions of workers in the most uncertain trades of this country — trades like shipbuilding, engineering, and building — to secure unemployment benefits, which in a great majority of cases will be sufficient to tide them over the season of unemployment. This scheme in its compulsory form is limited to certain great trades like those I have specified, but it will be open to other trades, to trade unions, to workers' associations of various kinds, or even to individuals to insure with the State Unemployment Insurance Office against unemployment on a voluntary basis, and to secure, through the State subvention, much better terms than it would be possible for them to obtain at the present time.

(iii) **Labour Exchanges.** It would be impossible to work a scheme of Unemployment Insurance except in conjunction with some effective method of finding work and of testing willingness to work, and that can only be afforded by a national system of Labour Exchanges. That Bill has already passed through Parliament, and in the early months of next year we hope to bring it into operation by opening, all over the country, a network of Labour Exchanges connected with each other and with the centre by telephone. We believe this organization may secure for labour — and, after all, labour is the only thing the great majority of people have to sell — it will secure for labour, for the first time, that free and fair market which almost all other commodities of infinitely less consequence already enjoy, and will replace the present wasteful, heart-breaking wanderings aimlessly to and fro in search of work by a scientific system; and we believe that the influence of this system in the end must tend to standardize the conditions of wages and employment throughout the country.

The Development Act. Lastly, in connection with unemployment I must direct your attention to the Development Act, the object of which is to provide a fund for the economic development of our country, for the encouragement of agriculture, for afforestation, for the colonization of England, and for the making of roads, harbours, and other public works. And I should like to draw your attention to a very important clause in that Bill, which says that the prosecution of these works shall be regulated, as far as possible, by the conditions of the labour market, so that in a very bad year of unemployment they can be expanded, so as to increase the demand for labour at times of exceptional slackness, and thus correct and counterbalance the cruel fluctuations of the labour market. The large sums of money which will be needed for these purposes are being provided by the Budget of Mr Lloyd George, and will be provided in an expanding volume in the years to come through the natural growth of the taxes we are imposing.

Relief of distress. I have hitherto been speaking of the industrial organization of insurance schemes, Labour Exchanges, and economic development. Now I come to that great group of questions which are concerned with the prevention and relief of distress. We have before us the reports of the majority and minority of the Royal Commission on the Poor Law, and we see there a great and urgent body of reforms which require the attention of Parliament. The first and most costly step in the relief of distress has already been taken by the Old-Age Pensions Act, supplemented, as it will be if the Budget passes, by the removal of the pauper disqualification. By that Act we have rescued the aged from the Poor Law. We have yet to rescue the children; we have yet to distinguish effectively between the bona fide unemployed workman and the mere loafer and vagrant; we have yet to transfer the sick, the inebriate, the feeble-minded, and the totally demoralized to authorities specially concerned in their management and care.

All these schemes are interdependent. But what I want to show you, if I have made my argument clear, is that all these schemes — which I can do little more than mention this afternoon, though each one of which is important — are connected one with the other, fit into one another at many points, that they are part of a concerted and interdependent system for giving a better, fairer social organization to the masses of our fellow-countrymen. Unemployment Insurance, which will help to tide a workman over a bad period, is intimately and necessarily associated with the Labour Exchanges which will help to find him work and which will test his willingness to work. This, again, will be affected by the workings of the Development Act, which, as I told you, we trust may act as a counterpoise to the rocking of the industrial boat and give a greater measure of stability to the labour market.

The fact that everybody in the country, man and woman alike, will be entitled, with scarcely any exception, to an Old-Age Pension from the State at the age of seventy — that fact makes it ever so much cheaper to insure against invalidity or infirmity up to the age of seventy. And, with the various insurance schemes which are in preparation, we ought to be able to set up a complete ladder, an unbroken bridge or causeway, as it were, along which the whole body of the people may move with a certain assured measure of security and safety against hazards and misfortunes. Then, if provision can be arranged for widows and orphans who are left behind, that will be a powerful remedy against the sweating evil; for, as you know, these helpless people, who in every country find employment in particular trades, are unable to make any fair bargain for themselves, and their labours, and this consequently leads to the great evils which have very often been brought to the notice of Parliament. That, again, will fit in with the Anti-Sweating Act we are passing through Parliament this year.

A stronger nation. Now, I want you to see what a large, coherent plan we are trying to work out, and I want you to believe that the object of the plan and the results of it will be to make us a stronger as well as a happier nation. I was reading the other day some of the speeches made by Bismarck — a man who, perhaps more than any other, built up in his own lifetime the strength of a great nation — speeches which he made during the time when he was introducing into Germany those vast insurance schemes, now deemed by all classes and parties in Germany to be of the utmost consequence and value. 'I should like to see the State,' said Prince Bismarck in 1881, 'which for the most part consists of Christians, penetrated to some extent by the principles of the religion which it professes, especially as concerns the help one gives to his neighbour, and sympathy with the lot of old and suffering people.' Then, again, in the year 1884 he said, 'The whole matter centres in the question, "Is it the duty of the State or is it not to provide for its helpless citizens?" I maintain that it is its duty, that it is the duty, not only of the "Christian" State, as I ventured once to call it when speaking of "Practical Christianity", but of every State.'

Self-reliance is stimulated by hope. There are a great many people who will tell you that such a policy, as I have been endeavouring to outline to you this afternoon, will not make our country stronger, because it will sap the self-reliance of the working classes. It is very easy for rich people to preach the virtues of self-reliance to the poor. It is also very foolish, because, as a matter of fact, the wealthy, so far from being self-reliant, are dependent on the constant attention of scores, and sometimes even hundreds, of persons who are employed in waiting upon them and ministering to their wants. I think you will agree with me, on the other hand — knowing what you do of the life of this city and of the working classes generally — that there are often trials and misfortunes which come upon working-class families quite beyond any provision which their utmost unaided industry and courage could secure for them. Left to themselves, left absolutely to themselves, they must be smashed to pieces, if any exceptional disaster or accident, like recurring sickness, like the death or incapacity of the breadwinner, or prolonged or protracted unemployment, fall upon them.

There is no chance of making people self-reliant by confronting them with problems and with trials beyond their capacity to surmount. You do not make a man self-reliant by crushing him under a steam-roller. Nothing in our plans will relieve people from the need of making every exertion to help themselves, but, on the contrary, we consider that we shall greatly stimulate their efforts by giving them for the first time a practical assurance that those efforts will be crowned with success.

A lifebelt. It is a great mistake to suppose that thrift is caused only by fear; it springs from hope as well as from fear; where there is no hope, be sure there will be no thrift. No one supposes that five shillings a week is a satisfactory provision for old age. No one supposes that seventy is the earliest period in a man's life when his infirmities may overwhelm him. We have not pretended to carry the toiler on to dry land; it is beyond our power. What we have done is to strap a lifebelt around him, whose buoyancy, aiding his own strenuous exertions, ought to enable him to reach the shore.

Is this effort to perish? I have now tried to show you that the Budget, and the policy of the Budget, is the first conscious attempt on the part of the State to build up a better and a more scientific organization of society for the workers of this country, and it will be for you to say — at no very distant date — whether all this effort for a coherent scheme of social reconstruction is to be swept away into the region of lost endeavour.

The family life of the masses is the only foundation for the State. People talk vaguely of the stability of society, of the strength of the Empire, of the permanence of a Christian civilization. On what foundation do they seek to build? There is only one foundation — a healthy family life for all. If large classes of the population live under conditions which make it difficult if not impossible for them to keep a home together in decent comfort, if the children are habitually underfed, if the housewife is habitually overstrained, if the bread-winner is under-employed or under-paid, if all are un-protected and uninsured against the common hazards of modern industrial life, if sickness, accident, infirmity, or old age, or unchecked intemperance, or any other curse or affliction, break up the home, as they break up thousands of homes, and scatter the family, as they scatter thousands of families in our land, it is not merely the waste of earning-power or the dispersal of a few poor sticks of furniture, it is the stamina, the virtue, safety, and honour of the British race that are being squandered.

To buttress the homes. Now the object of every single con-structive proposal to which the revenues raised by this Budget will be devoted, not less than the object of the dis-tribution of the taxes which make up the Budget, is to buttress and fortify the homes of the people. That is our aim; to that task we have bent our backs; and in that labour we shall not be daunted by machine-made abuse of partisans or by the nervous clamour of selfish riches.

Whatever power may be given to us shall be used for this object. It is for you to say whether power will be given us to prevail.

What is the alternative? A period of supreme effort lies before you. The election with which this Parliament will close, and towards which we are moving, is one which is different in notable features from any other which we have known. Looking back over the politics of the last thirty years, we hardly ever see a Conservative Opposition approaching an election without a programme, on paper at any rate, of social and democratic reform. There was Lord Beaconsfield with his policy of 'health and the laws of health'. There was the Tory democracy of Lord Randolph Churchill in 1885 and 1886, with large, far-reaching plans of Liberal and democratic reform, of a generous policy to Ireland, of retrenchment and reduction of expenditure upon naval and military armaments — all promises to the people, and for the sake of which he resigned rather than play them false. Then you have the elections of 1892 and 1895. In each the Conservative Party, whether in office or Opposition, was, under the powerful influence of Mr Chamberlain, committed to most extensive social programmes, of what we should call Liberal and Radical reforms, like the Workmen's Compensation Act and Old-Age Pensions, part of which were carried out by them and part by others.

The Conservative Party have no policy to offer. But what social legislation, what plans of reform do the Conservative Party offer now to the working people of England if they will return them to power? I have studied very carefully the speeches of their leaders — if you can call them leaders — and I have failed to discover a single plan of social reform or reconstruction. Upon the grim and sombre problems of the

Poor Law they have no policy whatever; upon unemployment no policy whatever; for the evils of intemperance no
policy whatever, except to make sure of the public-house
vote; upon the question of the land, monopolized as it is in
the hands of so few, denied to so many, no policy whatever;
for the distresses of Ireland, for the relations between the
Irish and British peoples, no policy whatever unless it be
coercion. In other directions where they have a policy, it is
worse than no policy. For Scotland the Lords' veto, for
Wales a Church repugnant to the conscience of the overwhelming majority of the Welsh people, crammed down
their throats at their own expense.

Except reaction. It would be bad enough if a party so
destitute, according to its own statement, of political merit
were to return with the intention of doing nothing but re-
peating and renewing our experiences under Mr Balfour's
late administration, of dragging through empty sessions, of
sneering at every philanthropic enthusiasm, of flinging a sop
from time to time to the brewers or the parsons or the landed
classes. But those would not be the consequences which
would follow from the Tory triumph. Consequences far more
grave, immeasurably more disastrous, would follow. We are
not offered an alternative policy of progress, we are not confronted even with a policy of standstill, we are confronted
with an organized policy of constructive reaction. We are to
march back into those shades from which we had hoped
British civilization and British science had finally emerged.

The social meaning of a tariff. If the Conservative Party
win the election they have made it perfectly clear that it is
their intention to impose a complete Protective tariff, and to
raise the money for ambitious armaments and colonial
projects by taxing the poor. They have declared, with a

frankness which is, at any rate, remarkable, that they will immediately proceed to put a tax on bread, a tax on timber, and an innumerable schedule of taxes on all manufactured articles imported into the United Kingdom; that is to say, that they will take by all these taxes a large sum of money from the pockets of the wage-earners, by making them pay more for the food they eat, the houses they live in, and the comforts and conveniences which they require in their homes, and that a great part of this large sum of money will be divided between the landlords and the manufacturers in the shape of increased profits; and even that part of it which does reach the Exchequer is to be given back to these same classes in the shape of reductions in income tax and in direct taxation. If you face the policy with which we are now threatened by the Conservative Party fairly and searchingly, you will see that it is nothing less than a deliberate attempt on the part of important sections of the propertied classes to transfer their existing burdens to the shoulders of the masses of the people, and to gain greater profits for the investment of their capital by charging higher prices.

Liberalism and labour. The fortunes and the interests of Liberalism and labour are inseparably interwoven; they rise by the same forces and in spite of similar obstacles, they face the same enemies, they are affected by the same dangers, and the history of the last thirty years shows quite clearly that their power of influencing public affairs and of commanding national attention fluctuate together. Together they are elevated, together they are depressed, and any Tory reaction which swept the Liberal Party out of power would assuredly work at least proportionate havoc in the ranks of labour. That may not be a very palatable truth, but it is a truth none the less.

The lesson from Germany. We are often told that there can be no progress for democracy until the Liberal Party has been destroyed. Let us examine that. Labour in this country exercises a great influence upon the Government. That is not so everywhere. It is not so, for instance in Germany, and yet in Germany there is no Liberal Party worth speaking of. Labour there is very highly organized, and the Liberal Party there has been destroyed. In Germany there exists exactly the condition of affairs, in a party sense, that Mr Keir Hardie and his friends are so anxious to introduce here. A great social democratic party on the one hand are bluntly and squarely face to face with a capitalist and military confederation on the other. That is the issue, as it presents itself in Germany; that is the issue, as I devoutly hope it may never present itself here. And what is the result? In spite of the great numbers of the Socialist Party in Germany, in spite of the high ability of its leaders, it has hardly any influence whatever upon the course of public affairs. It has to submit to food taxes and to conscription; and I observe that Herr Bebel, the distinguished leader of that party, at Mannheim was forced to admit, and admitted with great candour, that there was no other country in Europe so effectively organized as Germany to put down anything in the nature of a violent Socialist movement. That is rather a disquieting result to working men of having destroyed the Liberal Party.

But we are told to wait a bit; the Socialist Party in Germany is only three millions. How many will there be in ten years' time? That is a fair argument. I should like to say this. A great many men can jump four feet, but very few can jump six feet. After a certain distance the difficulty increases progressively. It is so with the horse-power required to drive great ships across the ocean; it is so with the lifting power required to raise balloons in the air. A balloon goes up quite easily for a certain distance, but after a certain distance it refuses to go up any farther, because the air is too rarified to float it and sustain it. And therefore, I would say let us examine the concrete facts.

Property in Britain very widely divided. In France, before the Revolution, property was divided among a very few people. A few thousand nobles and priests and merchants had all the wealth in the country; twenty-five million peasants had nothing. But in modern States, such as we see around us in the world today, property is very widely divided. Especially is that true in Great Britain. Nowhere else in the world, except, perhaps, in France and the United States, are there such vast numbers of persons who are holders of interest-bearing, profit-bearing, rent-earning property, and the whole tendency of civilization and of free institutions is to an ever-increasing volume of production and an increasingly wide diffusion of profit. And therein lies the essential stability of modern States. There are millions of persons who would certainly lose by anything like a general overturn, and they are everywhere the strongest and best organized millions. And I have no hesitation in saying that any violent movement would infallibly encounter an overwhelming resistance, and that any movement which was inspired by mere class prejudice, or by a desire to gain a selfish advantage, would encounter from the selfish power of the 'haves' an effective resistance which would bring it to sterility and to destruction.

Liberalism enlists hundreds of thousands upon the side of progress whom Socialism would drive into reaction. And here is the conclusion to which I lead you. Something more is needed if we are to get forward. There lies the function of the Liberal Party. Liberalism supplies at once the higher impulse and the practicable path; it appeals to persons by sentiments of generosity and humanity; it proceeds by courses of moderation. By gradual steps, by steady effort from day to day, from year to year, Liberalism enlists hundreds of thousands upon the side of progress and popular democratic reform whom militant Socialism would drive into violent Tory reaction. That is why the Tory Party hate us. That is why they, too, direct their attacks upon the great organization of the Liberal Party, because they know it is through the agency of Liberalism, that society will be able in the course of time to slide forward, almost pain-lessly — for the world is changing very fast — on to a more even and a more equal foundation.

The cause of Liberalism is the cause of the left-out millions. That is the mission that lies before Liberalism. The cause of the Liberal Party is the cause of the left-out millions; and because we believe that there is in all the world no other instrument of equal potency and efficacy available at the present time for the purposes of social amelioration, we are bound in duty and in honour to guard it from all attacks, whether they arise from violence or from reaction.

No man can be a collectivist alone or an individualist alone. No man can be a collectivist alone or an individualist alone. He must be both an individualist and a collectivist. The nature of man is a dual nature. The character of the organ-ization of human society is dual. Man is at once a unique being and a gregarious animal. For some purposes he must be collectivist, for others he is, and he will for all times remain, an individualist. Collectively we have an Army and a Navy and a Civil Service; collectively we have a Post Office, and a police, and a Government; collectively we light our streets and supply ourselves with water;

collectively we indulge increasingly in all the necessities of communication. But we do not make love collectively, and the ladies do not marry us collectively, and we do not eat collectively, and we do not die collectively, and it is not collectively that we face the sorrows and the hopes, the winnings and the losings of this world of accident and storm.

Collective organization and individual incentive. No view of society can possibly be complete which does not comprise within its scope both collective organization and individual incentive. The whole tendency of civilization is, however, towards the multiplication of the collective functions of society. The ever growing complications of civilization create for us new services which have to be undertaken by the State, and create for us an expansion of the existing services.

I am of opinion that the State should increasingly assume the position of the reserve employer of labour. I am very sorry we have not got the railways of this country in our hands. We may do something better with the canals, and we are all agreed that the State must increasingly and earnestly concern itself with the care of the sick and aged, and, above all, of the children.

Liberalism cannot cut itself off from the field of social effort. I look forward to the universal establishment of minimum standards of life and labour, and their progressive elevation as the increasing energies of production may permit. I do not think that Liberalism in any circumstances can cut itself off from this fertile field of social effort, and I would recommend you not to be scared in discussing any of these proposals, just because some old woman comes along and tells you they are Socialistic. If you take my advice, you will judge each case on its merits. Where you find that State enterprise is likely to be ineffective, then utilize private enterprise, and do not grudge them their profits.

The vigour of competition not to be impaired, but the cause and reasons of failure mitigated. The existing organization of society is driven by one main-spring — competitive selection. It may be a very imperfect organization of society, but it is all we have got between us and barbarism. It is all we have been able to create through unnumbered centuries of effort and sacrifice. It is the whole treasure which past generations have been able to secure, and which they have been able to bequeath; and great and numerous as are the evils of the existing condition of society in this country, the advantages and achievements of the social system are greater still. Moreover, that system is one which offers an almost indefinite capacity for improvement. We may progressively eliminate the evils; we may progressively augment the good which it contains. I do not want to see impaired the vigour of competition, but we can do much to mitigate the consequences of failure. We want to draw a line below which we will not allow persons to live and labour, yet above which they may compete with all the strength of their manhood. We want to have free competition upwards; we decline to allow free competition to run downwards.

Active Liberalism the indispensable factor in the noble evolution of society. We do not want to pull down the structures of science and civilization but to spread a net over the abyss; and I am sure that if the vision of a fair Utopia which cheers the hearts and lights the imagination of the toiling multitudes, should ever break into reality, it will be by developments through, and modifications in, and by improvements out of, the existing competitive organization of society; and I believe that Liberalism mobilized, and active

as it is today, will be a principal and indispensable factor in
that noble evolution.

**The Budget has been murdered — John Brown's body lies a-
mouldering in the grave, but his soul goes marching on.**
The Budget has been murdered. John Brown's body lies
a-mouldering in the grave, but his soul goes marching on.
A spirit of social service and of social justice, of a larger
brotherhood possible among men, of a conscious and concerted effort towards a better state of things. That spirit
lives to vivify and fortify our line of battle, and, I will add,
to purify and sanctify our cause. And wherever throughout
the land men and women are found doing their best for
their fellow-countrymen, willing to make exertions and
sacrifices for the causes of the weak and the poor, there we
shall find friends and comrades in this struggle; there we
shall find enthusiasms and resolves which will support us;
there we shall find an inexhaustible and boundless strength,
sustained by which we shall surely conquer now.

THE PEOPLE'S CHOICE

6 THE PEOPLE'S CHOICE

The money must be found. The money must be found. Sixteen millions extra have to be provided before March 31st of next year — for the expenses of 1909. The necessity of raising that money is undisputed. The objects for which it is required are legitimate. The merits of the expenditure are not challenged by any party or in any quarter of the country. The pensions have been granted. They must be paid for. The soldiers and sailors have been enlisted. They must be maintained. The ships have been ordered. They must be completed. Both the great parties are committed to the expenditure. The Conservative Party are even more committed to the expenditure than the Government. For they were the first to promise Old-Age Pensions, and when the Bill which we introduced was under discussion in the House of Commons it was the Conservative Party who endeavoured recklessly and irresponsibly to extend its scope. And as for the Navy, they are dissatisfied even with the great provision we have made, and they were lately endeavouring by means of a most mischievous panic to stir up alarm in the country and ill-will between this country and other great countries, and so to provoke a more extreme expenditure. There is no doubt about the need for the money. There is no doubt that the money has to be found. And the first question I ask you is — how is the money to be found?

Action will follow upon your choice. That is a question which raises the deepest and fiercest issues in our active and vehement national life. Two plans have been put before you for meeting this need, and at the election which is upon us, you will have to choose between the plans which are put forward — between the alternatives which are open. And you will choose in the light of this important fact: that by your choice you will be bound, and that immediately upon your choice, action will follow one way or the other. Because in the pass to which our politics have come neither party will be content with talking, and the result of the election will be swiftly followed by action, prompt action, one way or the other, to give effect to the decision of the electorate.

Our plan is a precise and definite plan. Our plan has been placed before you. We propose to raise this money by taxing luxuries, monopolies, and superfluities. Having accorded substantial relief to the poorer class of income-tax payers, we propose to raise the general rate of the income tax by twopence and we propose to impose a super-tax upon incomes of over £5,000 a year. We propose to raise a further levy from great estates when they are transmitted at death to a new occupant. We propose to come to the working classes boldly for a contribution on their whisky and on their tobacco. We felt sure that they would not resent paying their share as part of a large and fair arrangement; and we propose to raise further revenue from the special taxation of liquor licences — a valuable monopoly granted by the State on much too easy terms; on mining royalties, which escape a great many or all the obligations to which other forms of property are amenable; on land values, and on unearned increment from the monopoly of land. By these means we believe we shall be able to raise the money necessary for the service of the year. And more, the taxes which

we are imposing this year will yield an expanding revenue
for the increasing needs of the future. Our plan has been
stated in precise detail. There is no doubt about it. We have
put it into the words of a Bill. We have framed it in the
clauses and the chapters of a statute. It has been examined,
as no other similar plan has ever been examined in the
history of this country. The Government and their experts
have examined it and studied it. The country has studied
and examined it, and the House of Commons has spent
over six hundred hours in discussing and debating it with
full knowledge and with elected responsibility.

Vagueness of tariff policy. The other plan which is before us
is vague, it is concealed, it is uncertain. We catch a glimpse
of its glittering skirts in the flourish of a peroration. We find
some reference to it upon a half-sheet of note-paper. It
figures in the after-dinner speeches of irresponsible persons.
We try to follow it through the cryptic pronouncements and
laboured ambiguities of political leaders. We have it brought
to our notice by the puffs and paragraphs and trial balloons
of the inspired, or semi-inspired, or wholly imaginative
press. It has never been put forward more vaguely and less
boldly than in Mr Balfour's so-called manifesto, which we
have had the pleasure of reading this morning and of which
I will say that no more flat, mild, stale, muddy, and dis-
couraging beverage was ever handed out to a peculiarly
thirsty party on the eve of a great exertion.

The main features can be discerned. But vague as are the
features of that plan, certain outlines and objects emerge,
like the headlands coming out of the mists upon the sea
coast, which we can certainly measure and which we are
bound to reckon with. From these we see the main distinctions between the two proposals now before you for

raising the money. Ours is a Free Trade plan; theirs is a Protectionist, or, if they like, a Tariff Reformist plan. Our plan taxes wealth; their plan taxes wages. Ours taxes luxuries, theirs taxes prime necessities. Ours deals with incomes, estates, and land values; theirs with bread, meat, and manufactured articles. Vague as their plan is in some of its aspects, this issue stands out plain and stark, beyond doubt or misconception of any kind whatever, and it is upon this issue that, in the first place, you have got to make your choice.

The social justice point of view. Let me say a word from the point of view of democracy and of social justice. Capital wealth is increasing very rapidly. Accumulations of capital are growing from year to year with extraordinary speed, and with even momentum. The yield of the income tax in ten years has increased by certainly not less than 109 millions sterling a year. In the meanwhile the wages of 10,000,000 persons whose returns are collected by the Board of Trade have advanced only by £10,000,000 in the same period. When the figures of this year are completed the calculation would be even more unsatisfactory. Among 1,100,000 income-tax payers £109,000,000 more is divided — £100 a man — and among 10,000,000 wage-earners £10,000,000 more has been divided; that is to say, £1 a man. These figures have been stated by me on several occasions. They have never been answered; they have never been faced.

Protection will not produce the revenue needed. Sixteen millions have to be found. A ten per cent duty will not yield it. It might yield five millions or six millions. I doubt that. Even the great tariff of Germany, if you deduct petroleum, which we rightly classify as a raw material, only yielded three and a half millions from the taxation of all kinds of wholly or partly manufactured articles in the year 1907.

F

The taxation of bread and meat is proposed — 2s. a quarter on wheat and five per cent on meat. That would no doubt yield six or seven millions to the revenue.

Mr Balfour's pledges of remissions of taxation. But Mr Balfour pledged himself at Birmingham, as Mr Chamberlain has done over and over again, and he renewed his pledge at Manchester three weeks ago, that he would give back to the working classes in remissions of taxation upon sugar, tea, tobacco, and coffee whatever money was raised from the taxation of bread and meat. I ask again today, Do these pledges stand? Surely we ought to be told that. I anxiously read Mr Balfour's manifesto, which makes so very few things manifest, to learn the answer to a question of such grave importance. But not a word is said upon that subject. It will be quite open to Mr Balfour in the future to say, unless a further pledge is extorted from him: 'Look at my election address. I never renewed the promise in that. That was the formal and final statement I made to the country.'

He is silent about the Navy, and about paying for it. Mr Balfour says he is 'perforce constrained' to be silent about the Navy. That is a very good thing, I think, judging from the exhibition he made of himself at the beginning of the year, when he ran about the country with the March hares and April fools, endeavouring to create a wholly unfounded panic. I do not at all regret that he is 'perforce constrained' to be silent about the Navy. But I notice with less satisfaction that he is 'perforce constrained' to be silent also about paying for it. I distrust this silence upon a vital point. It is inconceivable at this juncture that these assurances would not have been repeated, if they had not been in jeopardy. And it may be that when having to choose between national bankruptcy — not being able to provide the revenue to meet the obligations of the State — between our taxes, which are the only way in which this money can properly and promptly be found, or, in the third place, failure to keep explicit public pledges — it is quite possible that Mr Balfour, having this ugly choice, this three-pronged trident, presented at his breast, may be 'perforce constrained' to take the line of least resistance and put a dead-weight charge upon the poor.

The weak, maudlin whine of selfish riches. Mr Balfour in his manifesto tells us that the super-tax frightens some and the death duties cripple others, and he raises the weak, maudlin whine of selfish riches. Why! it is only a few weeks ago that Mr Balfour repaired to the Albert Hall to say to the enthusiastic Primrose dames and knights who greeted him, 'The gigantic sacrifices which you will have to make in the next few years [for the Navy] must begin now.' It is a very quick change from that heroic attitude — from willingness to make gigantic sacrifices for a beloved country — to being frightened by the super-tax, crippled by the death duties. Judging by the figures which I have quoted to you it is clear where the main burden ought to be placed.

The homes of the people. But there is another far more important consideration than any one of figures. A certain minimum standard is necessary, if the head of a family is to be able to bring up children who will be valuable citizens of the State and if he is to maintain a decent standard of comfort. The mass of the workers in Lancashire enjoy that minimum standard and a good deal more. But there are also very great numbers who live near the line, and who have a hard struggle to make both ends meet. Sickness, infirmity, the death of the bread-winner — not extreme old age any more, I am glad to say — and protracted unemployment; all these hazards, when they occur, may shatter altogether the economy of a family, and may break up a home got together over many years. A large proportion of the homes of Britain are like vessels with low free-boards, water-logged. A very little and they founder, and the dark waters flow in and cover all. Any additional burden on the simple necessaries of life must have the effect of reducing the physical efficiency of the bread-winner, of weakening his strength, and of affecting the health of his children, and all of these consequences must have the effect of increasing the liability of each family to all those special evils of sickness, infirmity and death.

It is true food has gone up from natural causes, but that is an argument against Tariff Reform. 'You talk about cheap food,' say our Conservative friends. 'Food has gone up.' I am well aware that in recent years there has been a rise in food prices. It is due either to natural causes or to causes which are at present beyond the reach of statesmen. But at least we have the feeling that we are getting our food as cheap as the whole world can bring it to us, and if the general movement is towards higher food prices — and that seems to be the tendency all over the world — is that a reason for accelerating the movement? Is that a reason for aggravating a tendency which must unquestionably cause hardship? If food prices are rising from natural causes is there any need to add unnatural and artificial causes? That argument is an argument against and not for the proposals to tax food. We as a party take our stand with the utmost bluntness upon this subject. In our Budget we refuse to tax bread and meat. We add nothing to tea and sugar; on the contrary, the Government have greatly reduced the taxation upon sugar and somewhat reduced the taxation upon tea; and the only things we have thought it right to come to the working classes for are taxes upon their luxuries such as whisky and tobacco, which do not affect the physical efficiency of labour and do not necessarily affect the economy even of the humblest home. That is our policy. We know it to be sound and good. The choice rests with you, and we remit it with confidence to your hands.

A social policy. But we have a further policy. I said our Budget would pay the bill for this year. The great merit of the policy of my right honourable friend Mr Lloyd George is that he has for the first time, I think, in British financial history, looked ahead. Our policy pays the bill for this year, but it also provides an expanding revenue from the same taxes, without any further increase, for future years; and upon this expanding revenue we had intended, and I think I may say we still intend, to base a great policy of social reconstruction and reorganization. In the centre of that policy stands National Insurance against unemployment, sickness, infirmity, invalidity, and the death of the breadwinner — the same kind of great scheme of insurance which Bismarck gave to consolidate the structure of the social life of Germany.

One feature in that policy is the Labour Exchanges, which you will soon see in active operation, which Mr Balfour is good enough to praise very highly in his manifesto, but which he made no effort to establish during the many years in which his influence would have been decisive. Now the whole of this social programme, which I have no time this afternoon to develop but with which you are familiar and of which I spoke at length at Leicester and at Preston — a great coherent interdependent scheme to arrive at a better minimum standard of social life, and to safeguard even the poorest families against the common hazards which so often overwhelm them — stands or falls with the Budget. And here again the choice is with you.

The House of Lords and the constitutional issue. Now I leave the financial and economic issue and I come to an even graver subject. I mean the action of the House of Lords. I have been told by some of my Conservative friends in London you are making a great mistake to be so angry with the Lords for rejecting the Budget. The working classes, the electors in the country generally, the great mass of our citizens, they say, do not care about the constitutional issue. They will regard it, we are told, as mere House of Commons pedantry, to quote Mr Austen Chamberlain, or as the pet vanity of members of Parliament, to quote Mr Balfour. Well, gentlemen, during the last week I suppose I have addressed forty thousand people, and my impression, my profound and dominant impression, is that so far from not caring about the constitutional issue, they have scarcely cared to hear about anything else.

Shorter Parliaments. I am not at all angry that there is going to be a general election in January. The ground was never better. The union of the democratic forces was never more complete. We have never fought a battle with better prospects of fruitful victory. Besides, I am in favour of shorter Parliaments. I introduced a Bill when I was member for Oldham, or rather I tried to introduce a Bill in the late Parliament, to limit the duration of Parliaments to five years; but on the advice of Mr Balfour the Conservative Party incontinently rejected my plea to be allowed to have it read even a first time. I think Ministers have been quite long enough in power after four years, and certainly a five years' period would be sufficient. The Prime Minister, Mr Asquith, last night declared five-year Parliaments to be the policy of the Liberal Party, and an essential feature in any constitutional change which we shall undertake to make. I have always advocated, as you may have heard, that a dissolution should be sought from the Crown if the House of Lords rejected the Budget. I have advocated that even at times when very few believed that course would be taken. Don't let it be supposed that my charge against the House of Lords is that they have precipitated an appeal to the people. I like the appeal to the people. I dare say I shall like it a great deal better than they will. I have always considered that there are many party advantages in its coming at this time and upon these issues, and I am well content to have it so soon as may be found convenient in the ordinary working of our electoral system.

No right to force a dissolution. No; my charge against the House of Lords is wholly different from that. It is a three-fold charge. I charge them first with having exceeded their rights and duty in seeking to force a dissolution. Dissolution is the prerogative of the Crown. The House of Lords have never had any rights in regard to it under the Constitution. Secondly, they have meddled with finance, which is the sole concern of the House of Commons. They have intercepted and refused supplies which the Commons had provided to meet the requirements of the State. They have destroyed the Budget upon which your representatives, elected by your votes, have consumed a whole session of their life and strength. Thirdly, they have studied to aggrandize their position and by seizing the power over finance to make themselves predominant, if not indeed supreme, in the Constitution; and unless they are chastised for their temerity they will succeed in altering the whole balance of our political life.

No precedent. There is no precedent in the whole of English history for the rejection of the Bill which provides for the entire finance of the year. On the contrary, all the precedents are against it. In the year 1846, when Sir Robert Peel, contrary to the mandate he received, against the wish of the majority of his party, leaning upon the Opposition, carried the repeal of the Corn Laws — and thereby prejudicially affected for the time being the great estates, whose owners composed the House of Lords — even then the House of Lords did not dare to tamper with the measure. In the year 1895, when a Liberal Government was tottering upon the verge of the grave, and only succeeded in passing its Budget by fifteen or sixteen votes — a Budget which laid heavy burdens upon the Peers — even then they did not dare to touch it.

All the forms of Parliament are against them. All the forms of Parliament are against them. The special address made by the King to the House of Commons in the King's Speech in regard to supply; the fact that no estimates are made to the House of Lords, and that no financial statement is made to them; the fact that the House of Commons by its own offices always retains the custody of the Budget Bill after it has been passed by the House of Lords — all the forms of our Constitution which have grown up in hundreds of years clearly show that they had no right. Most clearly of all, the practical consequences of their action, the financial confusion and paralysis which is caused, the need of heavy and repeated loans to the great injury of trade which is caused by the deadlock created, shows that they were stepping entirely outside the already too wide limits which the Constitution had assigned to them.

Mr Balfour is seeking to alter the Constitution. The House of Lords are laying claim to new rights such as they have never enjoyed or dared to ask for before. Mr Balfour says in his manifesto that a single Chamber is impossible in finance.

This is the same Mr Balfour who only a year ago at Dumfries said, 'It is the House of Commons and not the House of Lords, which settles uncontrolled our financial system.' There is one of the flattest, nakedest contradictions in terms which has ever been recorded of the leader of a great party. Mr Balfour may have changed his mind, but the British Constitution does not change so quickly: it does not dance about with the exigencies of the party situation. Therefore, I say it is Mr Balfour who is seeking to alter the Constitution. It is he and Lord Lansdowne and their friends in the House of Lords who have begun the revolution. The great wheels have commenced to revolve. The Lords and the leaders of the Tory Party have set them in motion. Only the people can bring them to a full stop.

A claim to new rights. Let us look at the new powers which Mr Balfour claims for the House of Lords, and at which the House of Lords has already clutched for itself. The whole of civilized government depends upon finance. The control of the executive Government depends upon the power of the purse. The elected house has hitherto enjoyed the exercise of the power of the purse, and that is why the votes which you give, and which are all you have in politics, call into existence an assembly which chooses, regulates, and can change the excutive Government. Any division of the power of finance between the House of Commons and the House of Lords, any duality in the control over finance, means that the executive Government can no longer rest upon the House of Commons: it must rest, in part at any rate, upon the will and the pleasure of the majority in the House of Lords. That is a quarrel upon which the sword had been sheathed in triumph hundreds of years ago. The House of Lords now claim to make and unmake Governments; they claim the right to force a dissolution and to control finance.

Conservative candidates ask to be sent to the House of Commons to injure and degrade the House of Commons. Many Conservative members and candidates will be abroad in the next few weeks seeking the support of the electors to return them to the House of Commons. There is not one of them who endorses the action of the House of Lords who does not ask the electors to send him to the House of Commons for the express purpose of injuring and degrading the House of Commons. Mr Balfour says that the exercise of this new power which he claims for the House of Lords over finance, and which he denied them a year ago, will be rare. Murder is rare. But murder is punished, and perhaps it is because murder is punished, that it is rare.

There are some forms of power which, to be perpetually effective, do not require to be constantly used. The possession of this power over finance would force every Government to adapt its policy in all its branches, not merely in finance, to the special interests and special prejudices of the House of Lords.

The unrepresentative Lords. What is the character of the assembly which makes this prodigious claim? It is an hereditary assembly, it is non-elected; it is representative of no one; it is responsible to no one; it is permanent; it is irremovable except by its own act. All its members are of one class, and that, to quote Bagehot, 'not quite the best class'. Nearly all are of one party. To the extent of nine out of ten on most occasions, to the extent of five out of six on the average of the last forty years, they are an absentee assembly. Their action has been consistently partisan in the interests of the Tory Party. Who will challenge any one of these statements? They are not the language of controversy. They are statements which even the Conservative Party do not attempt to make head against. Even the Conservative

Party which, in the twenty years of its power, never thought of reforming the House of Lords, do not attempt to defend it as it is. But it is the House of Lords unreformed that has done the harm; and it is the House of Lords unreformed that we are going to deal with. Such an assemblage making such a claim is an affront to democracy. It is a dangerous attack upon your liberties which must be repelled by every man of spirit while life and strength remain in his body.

Stroke and counterstroke. The forward movement of the House of Lords has been curiously timed. It meets another movement already in full career. They have resolved to extend their veto over finance; we have resolved to restrict their veto over legislation. The Prime Minister in his speech last night said with a clearness none can mistake, and with a solemnity all should appreciate, that no Liberal Government will ever again take or hold office under the conditions which have prevailed in the Parliament which is drawing to a close. That is a statement which is binding upon every Liberal, official or unofficial alike, and if you support us the consequence of this declaration cannot fail to emerge in action after the election is concluded.

The position of the Liberal Government after four years of office. Where then do we stand today at the end of our fourth year of office? I put it plainly to you to consider, whether one is not justified in saying that we occupy a position of unexampled strength at the present time. The Government is strong in its administrative record, which reveals no single serious or striking mistake in all the complicated conduct of affairs. There have been no regrettable incidents by land or sea, and none of those personal conflicts between the high officials that used to occur so frequently under a late

dispensation. We have had no waste of public treasure and
no bloodshed. We are strong in the consciousness of a persistent effort to sweep away anomalies and inequalities, to redress injustice, to open more widely to the masses of the
people the good chances in life, and to safeguard them
against its evil chances. We also claim that we are strong in
the support and enthusiasm of a majority of our fellow-
countrymen. We are strong in the triumph of our policy in
South Africa; most of all we are strong in the hopes and
plans which we have formed for the future.

The time for words has passed. The time for words has
passed. We have now come into the realm of action, and it is
because we are in the region of action that we come to you,
and ask you to use your energies and power in the few weeks
that lie before us to secure for the Government an adequate
and overwhelming majority at the coming election.

The hope of modern industrial democracy is threatened. Do
not at this juncture choose wrongly. The advance of democracy towards better social conditions is very slow. A
great part of the nation live lives of harsh and exhausting
toil, cheered by few sunbeams of pleasure and darkened by
anxieties. A minority of our people, a minority numbered
by millions, suffers, I think, more acutely here in this civilized modern land than the Hottentots in their deserts or
the Eskimos on their ice-fields. Science alone strides stead-
fastly forward to the rescue, but science will not achieve
her work for this generation. The skies are stern above us.
But one conviction, a growing conviction, comforts and
fortifies the brave heart of humanity. We are, and we have
been for some years past, moving sensibly forward. Things
are getting better. We feel that we can make them better
still, even in our own time. We believe that we can make

them much better for the children who will tread the road when we are gone. That is the hope and the consolation here below — I do not speak of the consolations of religion — but that is the secular hope and consolation which fortifies and uplifts modern industrial democracy. Are you quite sure that the hope is not threatened now?

We are confronted with organized and aggressive reaction. We are confronted with organized and aggressive reaction. The policy of the Conservative Party is plain. In armaments a crushing burden, retorted on to other countries and retorted back from them with compound interest on ourselves; in international relations a desolating mistrust, marring the comity of Christendom; in trade a reversion to some at least of the barbarous delusions of the mercantile system; in taxation an attempt to tax the vital necessaries of life and to alter the social balance, to the detriment of the poorer classes. And in the Constitution, our ancient British Constitution, an effort to undermine the rights of the world-famed House of Commons and to exalt the privilege of an aristocracy no longer of valour, but of wealth. Between our country and these perils there are only your votes. But I think that they will be enough.

Do your duty at this historic crisis in the nation's history. These are the issues of the election: — The defence of your Free Trade system, the carrying of the Budget with the land and social reforms dependent upon it, and the settlement for ever of the evil, ugly veto of the Peers, which they have used so ill, so long. Believe me, if you work to that end, and if your labours are crowned, as assuredly they will be, with a full and ample measure of success, then in future times when your children ask you about the memorable events of the year 1910, you will be able to speak to them with confidence and with deep conscientious conviction that at a historical crisis in the nation's history you had done your duty.

The new and critical stage in the long story of our country. We have entered on a new and a critical stage in the long story of our country. Formidable forces and combinations surround us abroad. Grave problems vex us at home. We are responsible for the safe conduct of a gigantic Empire — the most wonderful association of States and peoples ever asembled since the Roman age under the headship of a single Crown. We are also responsible for the health, the peace, and the well-being of forty-five millions of people crowded together in these two small islands, and dependent from day to day upon the most complicated operations of industry, of commerce, and of science. The balance turns this way and that. What will be the consequences? Shall we bend or break under the burden which is imposed upon us? Or shall we rise in ever greater strength and force to the splendid labours with which Providence has entrusted us? A grand and united effort is needed; an effort to build up in our country, not a class civilization, but a national civilization; an effort to achieve for our people a life more serious in purpose, more thorough in organization, more equally shared, than any we have known, so that we may become in all the true and permanent elements of strength, a stronger people, and, far from the dangers of revolutionary violence, preserving contact with the famous past of our race, we may win for new generations of English men and English women the generous inheritance of a broader and a brighter age.

APPENDIX I

THE PRINCIPLES OF THE TRADE BOARDS BILL

From a speech on the second reading of the Trade Boards Bill
in the House of Commons April 28th, 1909

Sweated industries. Sweated industries — by which I mean trades where there is no organization, where wages are exceptionally low, and conditions subversive of physical health and moral welfare — cast dark shadows in what is, upon the whole, the growing and broadening light of civilization.

There is a clear reason for this which is in itself at once a justification for the special treatment which we propose for these trades, and a means of marking them off more or less definitely from the ordinary trades. In the case of any great staple trade in this country, if the rate of wages became unnaturally low compared to other industries, and the workers could not raise it by any pressure on their part, the new generation at any rate would exercise a preference for better pay and more attractive forms of industry. The gradual correction of depressed conditions over large periods of time is thus possible. But in these sweated industries there is no new generation to come to the rescue. They are recruited from a class rather than from a section of the community. The widow, the womenfolk of the poorest type of labourer, the broken, the weak, the struggling, the diseased — those are the people who largely depend upon these trades, and they have not the same mobility of choice, exerted, tardily though it be, by a new generation, but which is undoubtedly operative upon the great staple trades of the country. That is an explanation which accounts for the same evils being reproduced under similar conditions in different countries, separated widely from one another and marked by differences of general conditions.

Trade Boards. The central principle of this Bill is the establishment of Trade Boards, which will be charged with the duty of fixing a minimum wage. I am very anxious to give these Trade Boards the utmost possible substance and recognition. They will be formed on the principle of equality of representation for employers and employed, with a skilled official chairman or nucleus. That is the principle I have adopted in the new Arbitration Court recently established. That is the principle which will govern the system of Labour Exchanges, shortly to be introduced, and other measures which may come to be associated with Labour Exchanges, and I think it is an excellent principle.

The scope and powers of Trade Boards. At the same time, do not let us suppose that these Trade Boards will, in the first instance, be very strong or representative bodies. They are to be formed in trades mainly worked by women, where no organization has ever yet taken root, where there are as yet no means of finding and focusing an effective trade opinion. Where possible, they will be partly elective; in many cases they will, I expect, have to begin by being almost entirely nominated. In some cases it will be upon the official members alone that the main burden will fall. The work which we entrust to them wholly and finally is sufficiently difficult and important. We direct them by this Bill to prescribe minimum rates of wages. They are to find the minimum rate. For that purpose they are as well qualified as any body that we could devise. In this sphere their jurisdiction will be complete. The Board of Trade will not re-try the question of what is the right minimum rate. Another and quite different question will be decided by the Board of Trade. They will decide whether the minimum rate which has been prescribed by the Trade Board commands sufficient support in the trade to make its enforcement by inspection and prosecution likely to be effective.

Necessity for the probationary period. Now I come to the probationary period, and I know that there are a great many who have stated that it is mere waste of time. I, on the contrary, have been led to the opinion that it is vital to any practical or effective policy against sweating. It is no use to attempt in trades as complex and obscure as these with which we are dealing, to substitute outside authority for trade opinion. The only hope lies in the judicious combination of the two, each acting and reacting upon the other. A mere increase of the penal provisions and inspection would be a poor compensation for the active support of a powerful section within the trade itself. It is upon the probationary period that we rely to enable us to rally to the Trade Boards and to its minimum wage the best employers in the trade. In most instances the best employers in the trade are already paying wages equal or superior to the probable minimum which the Trade Boards will establish. The inquiries which I have set on foot in the various trades scheduled have brought to me most satisfactory assurances from nearly all the employers to whom my investigators have addressed themselves.

Agents relied upon for the enforcement of the Act. For the enforcement of this Act, and for the prevention of evasion and collusion, I rely upon the factory inspectors, who will report anything that has come to their notice on their rounds and who will make themselves a channel for complaints. I rely still more upon the special peripatetic inspectors and investigators who will be appointed under the Act by the Board of Trade, who will have to conduct prosecutions under the Act, and who will devote all their time to the purposes of the Act. These officers will incidentally clothe the Trade Boards with real authority, once the rate has been enforced, in that they will be responsible to the Trade Boards, and not to some powerful department of Government external to the Trade Board itself. I rely further upon the support of the members of the Trade Boards themselves, who will act as watch-dogs and propagandists. I rely upon the driving power of publicity and of public opinion. But most of all I put my faith in the practical effect of a powerful band of employers, perhaps a majority, who, whether from high motives or self-interest, or from a combination of the two — they are not necessarily incompatible ideas — will form a vigilant and instructed police, knowing every turn and twist of the trade, and who will labour constantly to protect themselves from being undercut by the illegal competition of unscrupulous rivals.

Wages of a sweated worker bear no accurate relation to ultimate price. The wages of a sweated worker bear no accurate relation to the ultimate price. Sometimes they vary in the same places for the same work done at the same time. And sometimes the worst sweating forms a part of the production of articles of luxury sold at the very highest price. We believe further, however, that decent conditions make for industrial efficiency and increase rather than diminish competitive power. 'General low wages', said Mill, 'never caused any country to undersell its rivals; nor did general high wages ever hinder it.' The employers who now pay the best wages in these sweated trades maintain themselves not only against the comparatively small element of foreign competition in these trades, but against what is a far more formidable competition for this purpose — the competition of those employers who habitually undercut them by the worst processes of sweating.

APPENDIX II

LABOUR EXCHANGES AND UNEMPLOYMENT
INSURANCE

From a speech in the House of Commons, May 29th, 1909

Main defects in modern industrial conditions. Two main defects in modern industrial conditions which were emphasized by the Royal Commission were the lack of mobility of labour and lack of information. With both of these defects the national system of Labour Exchanges is calculated to deal. Modern industry has become national. Fresh means of transport knit the country into one, as it was never knit before. Labour alone in its search for markets has not profited; the antiquated, wasteful, and demoralizing method of personal application — that is to say, the hawking of labour — persists.

The functions of Labour Exchanges. Labour Exchanges will give labour for the first time a modernized market. Labour Exchanges, in the second place, will increase and will organize the mobility of labour. But let me point out that to increase the *mobility* of labour is not necessarily to increase the *movement* of labour. Labour Exchanges will not increase the movement of labour; they will only render that movement, when it has become necessary, more easy, more smooth, more painless, and less wasteful.

I.   To organize existing employment. Labour Exchanges do not pretend to any large extent to create new employment.

Their main function will be to organize the existing employment, and by organizing the existing employment to reduce the friction and wastage, resulting from changes in employment and the movement of workers, to a minimum. By so doing they will necessarily raise the general economic standard of our industrial life.

II.   To supply information. So far as the second defect, 'lack of information', is concerned, a system of Labour Exchanges promises to be of the highest value. In proportion as they are used, they will give absolutely contemporary information upon the tendencies of the demand for labour, both in quality and in quantity, as between one trade and another, as between one season and another, as between one cycle and another, and as between one part of the country and another. They will tell the worker where to go for employment. They will tell him, which is scarcely less important, where it is useless to go in search of employment. Properly co-ordinated and connected with the employment bureaux of the various Education Authorities, which are now coming into existence in Scotland and in England, they will afford an increasing means of guiding the new generation into suitable, promising, and permanent employment, and will divert them from overstocked or declining industries. They will put an end to that portion of unemployment that is merely local or accidental in character.

Advantages of Labour Exchanges. They are the only means of grappling with the evils of casual employment with all its demoralizing consequences. They are capable of aiding the process of dovetailing one seasonal trade into another. A system of Labour Exchanges, dispensing with the need for wandering in search of work, will make it possible, for the first time, to deal stringently with vagrancy. And, lastly, Labour Exchanges are indispensable to any system of Unemployment Insurance, as indeed to any other type of honourable assistance to the unemployed, since they alone can provide an adequate test of the desire for work and of the reality of unemployment. The authority of both Reports of the Poor Law Commission may be cited upon these points; and I shall present this Bill to the House as an important piece of social and industrial machinery, the need for which has long been apparent, and the want of which has been widely and painfully felt.

Possibilities of the Exchanges. We hope that the Labour Exchanges will become industrial centres in each town. We hope they will become the labour market. They may, where necessary, provide an office where the Trade Board, if there is one, will hold its meetings. We desire to co-operate with trade unions on cordial terms, while preserving strict impartiality between capital and labour in disputed matters. It may, for instance, be possible for trade unions to keep their vacant-book in some cases at the Exchanges. The structure of those Exchanges may in some cases be such as to enable us to have rooms which can be let to trade unions at a rent, for benefit and other meetings, so as to avoid the necessity under which all but the strongest unions lie at the present time of conducting their meetings in licensed premises. The Exchanges may, as they develop, afford facilities for washing, clothes-mending, and for non-alcoholic refreshments to persons who are attending them. Separate provision will be made for men and for women, and for skilled and for unskilled labour. Boy labour will be dealt with in conjunction with the local Education Authorities; and travelling expenses may be advanced on loan, if the management of the Exchange think fit, to persons for whom situations have been found.

Unemployment Insurance. The policy of Labour Exchanges would be considerable if it stood alone; but it does not stand alone. As my right honourable friend the Chancellor of the Exchequer has announced in his Budget speech, the Government propose to associate with the policy of Labour Exchanges a system of Unemployment Insurance.

The four principles of the insurance system. Our insurance system will, in consequence, be based upon four main principles. It will involve contributions from workmen and employers; it will receive a substantial subvention from the State; it will be organized by trades; it will be compulsory upon all — employers and employed, skilled and unskilled, unionists and non-unionists alike — within those trades.

Trades to which system is to be applied. To what trades ought we, as a beginning, to apply this system of compulsory contributory Unemployment Insurance? There is a group of trades specially marked out for the operation of such a policy. They are trades in which unemployment is not only high, but chronic, for even in the best of times it persists; in which it is not only high and chronic, but marked by seasonal and cyclical fluctuations, and in which, wherever and howsoever it occurs, it takes the form, not of short time or of any of those devices for spreading wages and equalizing or averaging risks, but of a total, absolute, periodical discharge of a certain proportion of the workers. The group of trades which we contemplate to be the subject of our scheme are these: house-building, and works of construction, engineering, machine- and tool-making, shipbuilding and boat-building, making of vehicles, and millsawing.

Reasons for choice. That is a very considerable group of industries. They comprise, probably, at the present time, two and a quarter millions of adult males. Two and a quarter millions of adult males are, roughly speaking, one-third of the population of these kingdoms engaged in purely industrial work; that is to say, excluding commercial, professional, agricultural, and domestic occupations. Of the remaining two-thirds of the industrial population, nearly one half are employed in the textile trades, in mining, on the railways, in the merchant marine, and in other trades, which either do not present the same features of unemployment which we see in these precarious trades, or which, by the adoption of short time or other arrangements, avoid the total discharge of a proportion of workmen from time to time. So that this group of trades to which we propose to apply the system of unemployment insurance, roughly speaking, covers very nearly half of the whole field of unemployment; and that half is, on the whole, perhaps the worse half.

Scale of benefits aimed at. We propose to aim at a scale of benefits which would be somewhat lower both in amount and in duration of payments than that which the best-organized trade unions provide for their own members, but which, at the same time, should afford a substantial weekly payment extending over by far the greater part of the average period of unemployment of all unemployed persons in these trades.

Machinery of the scheme. The House will see the connection of this to the Labour Exchanges. The machinery of the insurance scheme has been closely studied, and, as at present advised, we should propose to follow the example of Germany in respect of Insurance Cards or Books, to which stamps will be affixed week by week. When a worker in an insured trade loses his employment, all he will have to do is to take his card to the Labour Exchange, which, working in conjunction with the Insurance Office, will find him a job or pay him his benefit.

The relation of the whole scheme of insurance to the present voluntary efforts of trade unions requires, and will receive, the most anxious consideration, and I am in hopes that we shall be able to make proposals which will absolutely safeguard trade unions from the unfair competition of a National Insurance fund, and will indeed act as a powerful encouragement to voluntary organizations which are providing unemployed benefit.

INDEX